W9-BWI-591

On Responsibility

Or

HERBERT

Responsibility

FINGARETTE

BASIC BOOKS, INC.,

PUBLISHERS

New York

London

Library of Congress Catalog Card Number: 67-28502
Printed in the United States of America
Designed by Loretta Li

Contents

On Responsibility

1 / Dimensions of Responsibility

In this book my topic is "responsibility." I explore such questions as: What is it to be a responsible person? When (and why) is a person said to be morally responsible *for* something? How does one become responsible? How is one to be excused from responsibility? In this first chapter I must make some over-all comments about the way I have gone about these explorations and about my results. My remarks here constitute, in effect, an attempt to *say* what in the other chapters I have in fact done. Without these remarks, the remaining chapters may appear to be *merely* a collection of independently published essays on quite a variety of topics. They do indeed constitute such a collection, but taken as a group they embody and exhibit certain fundamental theses regarding responsibility. What these theses are, and how they form a deep unity, I shall proceed shortly to say; the reader will, I believe, then easily see as he proceeds that the essays do exhibit the theses I shall here state.

A brief preliminary word is in order, however, as to my method. Why present a collection of essays touching on such various topics as psychiatry, Aeschylus, law, morality, and Confucius? As in the case of my previous book, the specific studies I include here are the record of explorations and discoveries as I pursued a road which, strangely, was always intuitively plain to me even though I could not have said where the road led or what was to be seen on the way. Reflecting upon the voyage, I have finally come to see in the large, and with a gratifying sense of discovery, where the road did lead and the significance of the detail seen along the way. In this chapter I report the now discovered meaning of the exploration. This chapter is thus the concluding chapter as well as the introductory one, and it should be read as such.

There are numerous ways to urge a philosophical thesis. One is argument, "proof." There are those who would say that something in the nature of argument is of the essence of a truly *philosophical* thesis. I do not agree. Argument for a thesis is one important philosophical instrument. Yet a philosophical point may be made by myth-making (Plato), aphorism (Nietzsche), purposeful sequences of examples (Wittgenstein), allusive exhortation (Kierkegaard), literature and drama (Sartre, Marcel), and by other ways of which some, no doubt, have not yet been invented. What is the essence of philosophy and whether my way of going about my investigations or presenting them is philosophical are questions I propose to bypass. I prefer not to be distracted from what I have to say in order to argue first the age-old and inexhaustible question of the essence of philosophy.

My approach is not that of lengthy argument on a single and high level of generality. It consists, instead, in conducting a series of intensive analyses of quite particular but paradigmatic problems in various special areas of human concern (psychology, ethics, law, religion, art). The weight of my largest theses, insofar as they do finally have weight, derives precisely from their mutually reinforcing and amplifying character even though they have emerged out of quite specific problems, each of independent interest, each studied in its own terms and to a good extent for its own sake. Thus, on the very highest level of organization, my theses draw their force from deep and careful soundings taken at very particular but strategic locations.

In my view, much that is essential and strategic for understanding the idea of responsibility has failed to receive adequate attention, especially in the contemporary work of English-speaking philosophers. Important as an understanding of the much discussed issues of "freedom" and "determinism" may be for an understanding of "responsibility," they do not by any means suffice. In this book I am concerned especially with two essential dimensions of responsibility: One is that of acceptance, of commitment, care, and concern, and of the attendant elements of choice and of the creativity in choice; the other dimension is that of the "forms of life," initially socially given and ultimately socially realized, which constitute the form and content of responsibility. Responsibility emerges where the individual accepts as a matter of personal concern something which society offers to his concern; the consummation of responsibility *may* include the transformation, in large or in small, of what was offered—but never consists in its mere nihilation.

Were there no pre-existent forms of life proffered to the individual *Homo sapiens*, the organism could never become truly human. But without acceptance by that individual, without his care and concern for a possible life as defined or suggested by his group, he becomes at best an intelligent and skillful outsider to humanity; he becomes, in the language of the psychiatrist, a "sociopath" or "psychopath," and in the language of the layman, "amoral," "perverse," "lacking humanity," or "shiftless" and "irresponsible."

Many of our most perplexing social and personal problems arise today because we make the usual (but no longer quite so trustworthy) assumptions that the individual is concernful and that society provides a possible structure and content for his concern. In the chapter on the Good Samaritan and American law, I have tried to show that the problem discussed there arises just because both these usual assumptions are untrustworthy. This chapter stands at a theoretical mid-point, however, and we had best begin now at the beginning.

In Chapter 2, I have tried not only to isolate and identify the dimension of acceptance and concern but to consider it in connection with a particular kind of individual, the psychopath. Since a substantial proportion of those who come to our criminal courts or to other agencies dealing with the "maladjusted" are psychopaths to a significant degree, the illustration in terms of which I explore the more general issue is itself of marked social importance today. The psychopath presents a financial problem for the public budget, a moral problem for the citizenry, and a legal-administrative problem of major dimensions for courts and mental hospitals. But the psychopathic personality poses acute problems at the personal level, too, for finally these people do have relatives, friends, business associates—all of whom suffer. Even where an individual is not clinically identifiable as a psychopath, the problem of lack of concern, of unwillingness to accept responsibility, is one which is, after all, ubiquitous in the lives of ordinary men as well as in the realms of literature, drama, and religion.

In Chapter 3, which deals with "dynamic insight" in psychotherapy, I have dealt in detail with still another kind of context where, in effect, acceptance of responsibility is a crucial element and yet is a perplexing one so soon as we try to elucidate with analytical precision just how and why it is crucial. In the discussion of therapeutic insight, we see the intimate links between accepting responsibility, choice, and practical understanding of socially given forms of conduct. In this chapter, as in each of the others, I have been concerned to treat the problem of the chapter in its own right as something of independent interest and as having many ramifications. I have tried not to *use* it and *manipulate* it so that it would merely serve to illustrate a previously held thesis. Indeed, I could not have done this, for the more general theses were, as I have said, the discoveries resulting from such exploring in depth.

Chapter 4, on the supposed distinction between real guilt and neurotic guilt, takes up the psychotherapeutic context again, but it does so from quite a different standpoint. Here I am concerned to bring out the *moral* unity of the person by arguing that "neurotic" guilt is not "pseudo" guilt but is genuine guilt having its source in acceptance by one part of oneself of what is in the main rejected by the person. Thus the troubles of neurosis are not illnesses, if by "illness" we mean a non-moral disturbance amenable to the therapist as mere technical expert; neurotic disturbances are forms of partial acceptance or rejection which, being only partial (and being rooted in self-deception), do pose special problems, but which nevertheless constitute moral disturbances rooted in evasion of responsibility.

Chapter 5 is a study of the *Oresteia* of Aeschylus. I suspect that at least one distinguished classicist took this essay to be an attempt to reduce the *Oresteia* to a psychoanalytical formula. This is an understandable misinterpretation of the point of the essay; there have indeed been too many instances of "explaining" literary works by reducing them to some psychological formula, and no doubt I did not dwell enough in my own essay on my own more general aims. I was, perhaps, too concerned with the specific point and not enough with methodological commentary. Nevertheless it was always absolutely explicit in my mind—and crucial to the whole enterprise—that I was essentially drawing certain parallels intended to throw light on the conceptions of psychoanalysis. I did, of course, wish to identify what I take to be *a* central theme of the *Oresteia*—the assumption of responsibility in the context of the individual's development. But to underline this theme, and to place it beside its psychoanalytic analogues, is not to reduce the whole of the *Oresteia* to the theme or to its analogues; it is, rather, to illuminate the latter by placing them within the far larger, richer context of the *Oresteia* as a whole. What is marvelous about the *Oresteia* from this standpoint is the amazing density of its tightly interrelated meanings: the religious, historical, social, moral, psychological, hortatory, and literary dimensions are like many facets of a gem, each reflecting what appears in the others until the whole seems to generate its own inner incandescence. Aeschylus is the teacher here. To single out some such theme as I have done and relate it to contemporary ideas is not to explain Aeschylus but to have learned from him a part of what he can teach us.

Not emphasized in my discussion, but nevertheless implicit in the earlier chapters, is the complementary aspect of acceptance—the "forms of life" which are ultimately the content of acceptance. This aspect is first explicitly brought out in the transitional chapter on the Good Samaritan and the Law. This chapter is directed to a quite particular problem of the American law—that of the passer-by or neighbor who does not come to the aid of someone evidently in dire straits. It is not surprising that we should introduce explicitly the element of the social content of responsibility in connection with a study of the law. The material in this chapter was originally presented to an international symposium which, in the same spirit as this book's methodology, was sponsored jointly by one of the more "philosophical" law faculties (the University of Chicago) and by an insurance company (Sentry). In the course of working out possible solutions to this problem it came to appear (to other participants as well as to me) that what was of the essence was not merely to call upon the citizen to accept his responsibility to help others in distress, but also to provide what at present we lack—an explicit social policy, defined and implemented in law and regulation, which gives content to the responsibilities of the concerned citizen. In this country, even the citizen who is ready to accept the role of Good Samaritan usually cannot know clearly enough the nature and bounds of his responsibilities: law and circumstance penalize the meddler at least as often as not.

To look back over the earlier chapters from the perspective of the Good Samaritan discussion is to appreciate that in each case there is the tacit presumption of forms of life which are possibilities proffered to the individual for acceptance by him. Insofar as accepted by him, these forms of life become then the substance of his own individuality; in turn the proffered world is thus sustained and reinspired by this dedication of his individual life force to the responsible living of these forms of life. The ideal representation of the success of this interaction is the *Oresteia;* here the subjective crisis of Orestes' accepting of responsibility, and the objective crisis of a cosmos of Law, Gods, and men whose fate awaits Orestes, are but two aspects of one event.

As one moves backward from the *Oresteia,* through the chapters on guilt, on dynamic insight, and finally the chapter devoted explicitly to the role of acceptance and concern, the emphasis is increasingly upon the "subjective" element, acceptance. But as one proceeds forward from the transitional chapter on the Good Samaritan to the chapter on Confucius, the emphasis shifts to the other extreme. The Confucian material of the last chapter underlines the social forms as the essence of humanity. It is not that Confucius denies or is blind to the necessity for acceptance and concern; it is simply that his attention is primarily directed to teaching *what* it is that must be accepted, and what are the consequences of such acceptance. Though I have not dwelt upon it in this particular essay on Confucius, he repeatedly emphasizes that one must love the good, one must dedicate oneself to the given forms of life in the world (*Li*), that without acceptance and concern for *Li,* one's native energies remain uncivilized, one's humanity aborted.

When the teaching of Confucius is brought into proximity to the teaching of such contemporary philosophers as Austin and Wittgenstein, as is done in this chapter on Confucius, one sees more distinctly how acceptance can emerge only in the medium of the given forms of life. Both Austin and Confucius, each in his way, teach that it is senseless to talk of acceptance independently of the forms of life (which include the forms of language) without which one could not intelligibly, effectively accept anything.

In truth, acceptance, commitment, concern are aspects of what, from a different vantage point, may be seen as conduct which realizes in the concrete the possibilities defined by the socially given forms. It is, one discovers, a matter of emphasis and not of separate existence—it may be the emphasis of the agent, who on occasion finds either the issue of acceptance or the question of the content of what he accepts more focal to his struggles, or it may be the emphasis of the analytical observer, who for his own theoretical purposes explores one or another of these aspects at a particular time.

If I were to set the matter out on a kind of linear scale, as I have in effect done by virtue of the chapter order of these essays, I would place the chapter on acceptance of responsibility at one end of the scale, the chapter on Confucius at the other end. In the middle I would place, preferably one above the line and one below, the *Oresteia* and the Good Samaritan; the former as a perfect revelation of a harmonious union of the two extremes, the latter as an infinitely more humble expression of an important contemporary breakdown for lack of elements from both ends of the scale.

I think it is helpful to use the image of the line whose two extremes represent what are apparently opposites but are in fact complementary aspects of one thing. Yet it is obviously only an image. Neither in this nor in subsequent chapters have I tried to define "responsibility" or any of its grammatical variants. Nor have I attempted to set forth a precise formula, an elaborate doctrine, or a definitive analysis as to what responsibility "is" or what the word "responsibility" means. It is my opinion that we deal here with one of those root notions, one not to be explained by translation into other terms but itself used in order to understand and to explain human existence. It is a root constitutive element of our idea of humanity and of what it is to be a person. Therefore one can say what responsibility is only to those who already have at least some practical, working understanding of it. And to "say what it is" amounts to sharpening and deepening this pre-existent practical understanding by selective allusion to contexts, circumstances, problems, or concepts which in varying ways exhibit in exceptionally vivid or critical fashion the dimensions of the idea of responsibility or of the quality of life lived responsibly.

I think there is a third major dimension of responsibility, one which I have not in any explicit way treated in these essays, one whose study also leads us to the very core of responsibility. This third dimension is that of obligation. The notion of obligation is the essential mediating one between that of acceptance and that of the proffered life-forms which are accepted. That "obligation" does have such an essential mediating role may be seen, or at least glimpsed, as follows.

To accept, in the sense of acceptance which I use in these essays, is obviously not merely a matter of physical grasping; and of course there may be no physical grasping at all involved. It is a move which gathers itself in the psychological, the subjective realm, but comes to full existence in the moral realm. One cannot understand acceptance, concern, commitment, as I have talked of them, without already having a practical understanding of obligation. To accept *is* to obligate oneself. Nor could one understand the notion of "forms of life" if one had not already a practical understanding of obligation. "Forms of life" is not a descriptive, "sociological" concept, not a reference merely to how people do behave, but a reference also to how they obligate themselves to act and how they pass judgment on their failure or success in carrying out their obligations.

Of course obligations are not entities which subsist independently in some metaphysical realm, entities to be grasped or rejected. "Obligation" is an abstract notion which is unintelligible independently of the idea of the forms of life which, in actual life, provide the content of particular obligations. Nor is "obligation" intelligible without a practical understanding of acceptance and concern. As I argue at length in the next chapter, it is pointless to talk of obligations where in truth the individual does not accept any responsibility.

We can speak intelligibly of responsibility when we have a situation characterized by the emergence of obligation-relations rooted in given forms of life, at times flowering into new forms of life, but nourished by individual acceptance and concern. There is a conceptual circularity latent here, but I believe the formulation to be philosophically illuminating—especially when elaborated by concernful reference in detail to the quite particular problems and circumstances of a civilization. I have concentrated in these essays on only two of the three dimensions, for I think that these two have been unduly ignored in contemporary philosophical discussion. The notion of obligation (and its close variants) has already received much attention in the analytical philosophical literature, but our philosophical understanding of it has been truncated, if my claims in this book are sound.

2 / Acceptance of Responsibility

I

In what one might call broadly the "English analytical tradition" in philosophy, there are many references to "moral responsibility." Yet, only rarely does one find any close examination of this notion. This is a noteworthy lack, since the notion would seem, *prima facie*, a crucial one for understanding the moral life. I would like to begin my discussion by suggesting one reason for this neglect. The reason is this: there has been tacit agreement about what the "elements" of any analysis of "moral responsibility" would be; and it is to these elements, rather than to the primary notion itself, that analytical attention has been directed. The upshot of my argument here will be that this tacit agreement is a mistaken one, mistaken by virtue of omission. Certain quite fundamental features of moral responsibility have been almost totally ignored. In turning here to a direct examination of "moral responsibility," I hope to show the relevance of some of these hitherto neglected features. I shall also examine them in themselves just enough so that we can identify them with reasonable confidence.

Let us summarily review the situation, then, first by identifying those features of moral responsibility which have been generally noted, and then by sketching in the hitherto neglected ones to be more carefully studied in the remainder of my remarks.

By some philosophers, moral responsibility is supposed to hinge upon certain aspects of the character and circumstances of action ("Did he do it?" "Is all behavior 'determined'?" "Was he free?" "Did he know what he was doing?" "Did he intend to do that?" "Could he have helped doing it?" "Are there any excusing or mitigating circumstances?"). Other philosophers hold that moral responsibility hinges on the answerability and deserts of a person ("Does he deserve punishment?" "Will blaming him alter his character or conduct?" "May he be called upon to answer for what happens?"). Still other philosophers have supposed that moral responsibility turns in some way on a combination of the preceding issues ("Did he do it in such circumstances as to be answerable for it?" "Shall we hold him answerable, ascribe responsibility to him, and in that sense say it was his action?"). Finally, it has also been argued that "moral responsibility" is a vacuous notion. This latter point of view, however, is usually a conclusion derived from analyses which are based on the presumption that only action or answerability or some combination of these are of the essence.

The problems associated with these and with closely related questions are more than sufficient to occupy a philosopher's full attention, and this is for the most part what they have done whenever the question of moral responsibility has come up.

It is not my purpose to proceed any further with discussion of "action" and "answerability." Instead, I shall devote myself to showing how a fuller understanding of "moral responsibility" takes one into quite different regions. In moving into these new regions, we shall come much closer to the continental divide of morality, what Kant called "the extreme limit of moral inquiry," the question why men should will the moral law. In approaching this extreme limit, Kant noticed, or thought he noticed, the following:

> When we present examples of honesty of purpose, of steadfastness in following good maxims, and of sympathy and general benevolence even with great sacrifice of advantages and comfort, there is no man, not even the most malicious villain (provided he is otherwise accustomed to using his reason), who does not wish that he also might have these qualities.[1]

Kant's assertion looks like an empirical generalization. Is it in fact true? Is it, perhaps, necessarily true? Shall we consider the unnerving possibility that it is false? And let us remember: we are concerned here with an individual "otherwise accustomed to using his reason," not with someone who is mentally ill or defective.

Let us, then, try to imagine an individual who knows what he is doing and, specifically, knows how it is considered from a moral standpoint. He is not coerced or under the sway of some powerful passion or intoxicating drug; he intends to do what he does, and he does it. Out of a casual not an "irresistible" impulse, he sets fire to a neighbor's wooden building. It's a fine spectacle, and he enjoys it.

Is he morally responsible for what he has done? Not necessarily. It is clear that, at least in certain kinds of cases, the ascription of responsibility is either dubious or inappropriate. We can begin by taking an easy but illuminating "out." Suppose the individual were a five-year-old who had obtained matches and who enjoyed playing with inflammables. He set the conflagration not out of spite or rebellion or malice, but for the pleasure of it. He knew it would lead to a destructive fire. He knows it is considered to be wrong, whether or not he gets caught, but he does not care about that; he cares only about the fire. The adult who had left the matches lying around might be held morally or even legally responsible. But the child, though he may be "taught his lesson," is not morally responsible.

Well, then, when will the child become, morally speaking, a man? He must be "of age." What age is that? The "responsible age" morally is not necessarily the legally "responsible age." A seventeen-year-old would be morally responsible for the same act, yet he would not be a responsible party before the law.

Is there an earlier birthday which of itself establishes that the individual is morally responsible? Does the fact that one has done something *and* is of a certain chronological age make one morally responsible? Surely mere chronological age has no such decisive moral role (though it does have such a decisive legal role, and that is one of the ways in which the law is admittedly arbitrary). Age is a simple and often dependable indicator of something crucial in connection with responsibility; but what is this something crucial that it indicates?

The gist of the answer is this: The individual is by a certain age expected to accept responsibility. And this acceptance is manifest—if it is genuine—in care (or concern), that specific kind of care which is peculiar to moral responsibility. There are many marks of such concern: inner moral conflict, self-restraint, remorse, guilt, as well as its more direct expression in taking care of that which one is responsible for.

Now what if this acceptance of responsibility and responsible care do not appear in the individual after he has "grown up"? What if Kant's assertion were false, or even if it could be conceived to be false? What if we found some "malicious villain," otherwise rational, who did not wish for or respect those noble qualities Kant mentioned? Such a man would not be morally "blind"; our "malicious villain" would be very knowledgeable about moral issues.

Of course we might argue, as a long line of philosophers from Socrates to Ryle have in fact argued, that to know the right is to do the right, or that "knowing" the right somehow "locks in" with "caring."[2] If we take this tack, we could say that our malicious villain (and the child) do not "really" know the moral character of their conduct. Helpful as this approach is, it nevertheless suffers by putting the whole matter into the wrong perspective for our purposes. It de-emphasizes acceptance and care by placing them in the shadow of that glamorous hero of the philosophic tradition, "Knowing." This, in effect, reinforces the previously mentioned tendency to neglect accepting and caring; it hinders us from seeing them as essential, distinguishable things we must do in order to achieve responsibility. A different angle of vision is needed.

Of course a "tough-minded realist" would take the view that we do not have to wait upon Smith's accepting moral responsibility for what he does. What an easy way out that would be! Unless Smith has one or another of the acceptable sorts of excuses, he is responsible for what he does.

No doubt the "tough-minded" case is plausible; but I take issue with it. I maintain that, were we to be convinced Smith really had not accepted moral responsibility, that he really did not care in the appropriate way, we would neither in justice nor in fact hold him morally responsible. And I shall begin the systematic presentation of this thesis by presenting some extreme and clear-cut illustrative material from the practical world.

II

There are persons—many of them—who do not accept responsibility, who care not at all, but who are otherwise healthy and rational. I have in mind those individuals most commonly known under the rubric "psychopathic personality," though they are now officially described as "antisocial personality" or "sociopaths." These are medico-legal labels. Let us not be put off by them. Let us not think of what might be the cause of such a person's troubles; let us look at what he is and does.

Here is a summary characterization, though still a somewhat lengthy one, of the psychopath. I have drawn directly from a classic text on the subject,[3] and I have woven directly quoted phrases with my occasional paraphrases into a running text.

> Alert, friendly, easy to talk with, he seems to have many genuine interests. No "nervousness"; nothing at all "off" or queer about him; poised. Frequent evidence of sound reasoning, often of superior intelligence. Not classifiable as

psychotic or neurotic; a common diagnosis after psychiatric examination: "no nervous or mental disease: psychopathic personality." Shows no evidence of defect in *discussing* complex matters of judgment involving ethical, emotional, and other evaluational factors. Capable of carrying out complex schemes and projects with success when he wishes.

His feelings are various and can be strong, but are evanescent and "superficial": Vexation, spite, quick and labile flashes of quasi-affection, peevish resentment, shallow moods of self-pity, puerile attitudes of vanity, absurd and showy poses of indignation are all within his emotional scale; however, mature, wholehearted anger, true or consistent indignation, honest, solid grief, sustaining pride, deep joy, genuine despair are reactions not found.

Does not show ordinary responsiveness to special consideration, kindness, or trust. Can act appreciative if he has a selfish aim; may show small courtesies, acts of generosity, helpful gestures either with ulterior purpose or on impulse; may equally well, on impulse, act in contrary fashion. A glib "actor"; lies often and easily. Generally skilled at social graces, which may be abandoned without evident reason. No enduring personal relationships based on affection or trust. Casual sexual relations; egocentric. Though glib protestations of responsibility and remorse may be used to influence others, insincerity is soon evident. No concern with either personal pride or more general esthetic or moral standards. Often drinks too much, though some psychopaths do not. Often, however, his behavior with little or no drink is much like that when drunk.

The psychopath, in the typical case (of which there are many), is constantly getting into trouble with neighbors, "friends," family, and police. Periods of socially acceptable conduct alternate erratically with destructive pranks, petty thefts, forgeries, fights, intoxication, miscellaneous other minor and often pointless crimes. Inexplicable minor cruelties, humiliations, inconveniences are dealt out freely by him. He knows the probable consequences of his acts, social and antisocial, but does not care—very often does not care even enough to try to protect his liberty by concealing his doings; he has no pride to protect.

In one case, for example, a twenty-year-old had been arrested and jailed over fifty times; except for the constant intervention and restitution on the part of his parents, he would have been in detention an estimated 150 times more. A characteristic bit of psychopathic conduct: the young man abandons his ill mother in a stranded car at night. Questioned later, he is entirely unembarrassed: on his way walking to the gasoline station, he met an acquaintance and got into conversation; as for his mother, "everybody has to die sometime."

The psychopath is Kant's "malicious villain" except that: (*a*) contrary to Kant's supposition, the psychopath has no wish for those qualities which would make a moral man of him; he will not accept responsibility; he does not care; and (*b*) necessarily, he is not consistently a malicious villain, for this would require an abiding concern, which is precisely what he does not have.

It would be misleading to call the psychopath morally incompetent or morally blind. He can, if he wishes, carry on a most intelligent, "insightful," and persuasive moral discussion. At times he very convincingly expresses "remorse" or "moral conversion"—though he may concurrently remain actively engaged in his usual conduct. If this performance is exposed, he is quite unembarrassed, since for him there is nothing morally at stake. He does not care; hence no shame.

What can one do with such a person? Well, what *do* people do? After all, the psychopath is not a rarity. Those who are psychopaths or who have psychopathic tendencies are now recognized to constitute a significant proportion of the social troublemakers handled in our courts, jails, and hospitals. The usual first response to him is what we should expect: those around him try to hold him responsible. His glibness and apparent sincerity, his social skill and his ability to get his friends and parents to make restitution for him usually lead to light punishment or to forgiveness for his misdemeanors. Eventually, those who have followed his career—parents, friends, police—come to appreciate that he is incorrigible. The cumulative effect of his antisocial acts, or perhaps some more flagrant criminal venture, brings him into court on a serious charge. If the opportunity for probation or dismissal by a skillful show of contrition will no longer do, his defense takes a radical turn. Now he has no compunction about bringing up his long, sorry record and using it as a basis for a plea based on "insanity." The fashions of our times and the procedures of the law both work to encourage the typical verdict: not guilty by reason (it is presumed) of insanity. He is then remanded to a psychiatric institution. There he is examined, and soon he is released because they have found: "no nervous or mental disease."

Now the psychopath is free to go the same round again, and he does so. The courts and juries generally cannot see their way to holding him responsible; the psychiatrists usually agree he is not insane according to the law. He is neither "ignorant of the nature and quality of his act" nor of right and wrong; even the hypothesis of "irresistible impulse" cannot be plausibly invoked.

To call this a "neurotic character disorder," as some psychiatrists do, is not to change any of the facts but to obscure the moral issue. For we have not discovered a defect in the "substratum" or the "machinery" of the will which *causes* the man to act as he does: we have simply observed what he does. Even if we discovered some relevant aberration "in the unconscious" or in the "machinery of the mind," this would merely give us further reason not to hold the person responsible. But we have enough reason without it. Anyone who conducts himself this way, whatever the reason, or even if there be no reason at all, is not morally responsible. If he simply will not accept responsibility and really does not care, then whatever the reason for his attitude, he has effectively made it pointless to consider him or to treat him as genuinely morally responsible. And as a practical matter, this is how we do respond to such cases.

It is, I would maintain, the inability to distinguish this question of acceptance of responsibility and responsible concern which has led to the persistent debate in psychiatric and in legal circles over the critical problem of classification and treatment of the psychopath. That there is such persistent debate over the limits of legal responsibility in this context, and that, specifically, the category "psychopath" remains the hard, indissoluble core of controversy—all this is evidence that the traditional doctrines are conceptually inadequate to the problem. In effect, these doctrines imply that the individual must be either responsible or mentally ill.

The reader will no doubt recall individuals of his own acquaintance who are more or less "irresponsible." They need not be all-around psychopaths. They may be in a number of respects reasonably mature. Yet, at least in some of their affairs, they have no sense of "responsibility." They do not seem to care. They may care about what pleases them; yes, in that sense of "care" they do care. But that, as we shall have occasion to note later, is not the kind of caring that counts. Perhaps we or others have tried to reform them. When at last we have fully appreciated their failure to accept responsibility, their moral carelessness, we throw up our hands. For practical purposes, we admit there is no point in treating these people as morally responsible in the areas of their life which are in question. Usually we miss the philosophical lesson we could learn. We postulate some standard excusing condition too well hidden for our eyes —the "unconscious" is always handy. Or else we acknowledge that "you can lead a horse to water but you can't make him drink"—and then we smile at our naïve reliance on such an old-fashioned view of the matter, thus failing to see how truly apt it is.

III

I would like to examine separately, now, and in greater detail, the notions of "accepting" and "caring" as used in the present context. Then I shall turn again to "moral responsibility," and shall, for the first time, consider various distinguishable ways in which we use that phrase and its close variants. First, then, we examine "accepting," after that, "caring," and finally around again to "moral responsibility."

A tobacco executive may "refuse to accept responsibility." He has no concern for the ultimate effects of the firm's vigorous efforts to establish the smoking habit among the young, to sell more cigarettes to those already habituated, and to inhibit public awareness of the medical evidence for the unhealthfulness of cigarettes. Nevertheless, though the executive may sincerely deny having accepted the responsibility to which we would hold him, we may reject his denial as not decisive. No doubt a fair-minded judge will find difficulties in achieving a final resolution of the question. But the executive's denial does not dispose of the matter. The question of the "acceptance of responsibility" is not that simple.

Certainly explicit statement of acceptance is not necessary. "Martha, will you marry me?" And Martha blushes, sighs, throws herself wordlessly into your arms, and embraces you rapturously. It will be a specious defense later if she argues, "But I never *said* 'yes.' " Acceptance usually needs no special words—only an intelligible history of act and circumstance.

There are times when one does accept responsibility by uttering some characteristic "performatory" utterance of the sort, "I accept responsibility for . . ." But these are occasional and special forms of acceptance, and they get their force, as I shall indicate later, from a commoner and tacit form of acceptance.

I have said that acceptance of responsibility may be and usually is tacit, but we should not confuse tacit acceptance with mere "natural growth" into a new moral state. This common error results in part from the fact that usually acceptance of responsibility is inextricably embedded in a long history of complex patterns of conduct. The responsibilities which are thus accepted may be—but need not be—earth-shaking ones. Yet in our self-consciously philosophizing moments, we easily tend to overlook the acceptance as such because it is not localizable in some single act or well-defined course of conduct.

For example, I am morally culpable if I do not show up for dinner, have given my wife no forewarning, remain away until late, and cause her grief and anxiety. I am responsible for being home reasonably promptly. Yet I never explicitly announced I would be home for dinner on this night, nor did I ever make some explicit but general commitment to the effect that I would always be home for dinner. I just do come home every night for dinner, and though this, considered in isolation, establishes no responsibility, taken in connection with other features of my home life, it all adds up to the fact that I have accepted this responsibility.

Why should I speak of "acceptance" here? Should I not rather say I just "become" responsible? To see why it is appropriately and enlighteningly called "acceptance," one must consider the following. At any point in my domestic career I could have acted otherwise than I did, often without betraying any of my responsibilities at the time. Had I acted differently, my responsibilities would often have had a different form. I might not have married domestic Martha and chosen doting Mary instead: she would have encouraged me to indulge myself. I might well have not married at all. I might have married Martha but only after we had "had it out" quite frankly: so far and no further would I go in the domestic regularities she was inclined to expect. Or I could have arranged that if I were not home by an hour before dinner, I would not be expected.

In short, I not only could have, of my own free will, handled my affairs differently, but in doing so I would have knowingly taken on other responsibilities than I did. Even more to the point: it is often the case that I decide as I do precisely in order to take on, or in order not to take on, certain responsibilities. Thus it is a natural and proper expression to say that *in* doing such and such, I accepted certain responsibilities; or to say that I would not do some other thing because I did not wish to accept the responsibility.

Of course tacit acceptance—and, for that matter, explicit acceptance—requires a certain mastery of the practices of men. I must know what I am doing—though I do not have to think of it consciously or be perfectly clear about it. How much one must know is a question to which we will return later.

A certain resistance to the idea that acceptance is necessary to responsibility no doubt has its roots in child-rearing practices. With children, our interest is to make them aware, for the first time, of the nature of the responsibility they ought to accept, and to educate them to accept that responsibility. (Even the "ought" in the preceding sentence has a special sense because it applies to one who is not yet a responsible individual.) It is a characteristic technique of education for moral responsibility that when the individual is judged "ripe" for accepting responsibility, we treat him much as if he had already done so. We praise, censure, appeal, "obligate," or "hold responsible." And it is in the nature of the human being that, if we have chosen our moment well, he usually responds to this treatment by actually accepting responsibility. We must carefully distinguish this use of "responsibility," in the pedagogical context, for here we do use it intelligibly before there ever has been an unambiguous acceptance of responsibility. Yet through it all, we withhold our judgment that the child is genuinely morally responsible until—until, I maintain, we see the signs that he has at last in truth accepted it.

IV

In turning to examine "care" and "concern," we shall not have left behind the aspect of acceptance. They are inextricably connected. We fully understand acceptance of responsibility only if we also understand its necessary expression in responsible care. And we understand *responsible* care not as an autonomous kind of comportment, not as whim, or taste, or liking, or affection, but as an aspect of the acceptance of responsibility. "Acceptance," "care," and "responsibility" are part of a family of terms which form a quasi-autonomous "language"; it is in the context of this language and its use that the terms take on the distinctive significance in question. Nevertheless, as in the case of "acceptance," we can find our way to the quite special sense which "care" has in the context of moral responsibility by picking up the spoor in neighboring contexts where "care" is used in related ways.

We have all had it happen to us, perhaps most often when we were youngsters, to try to "get up" a game with someone who, at least at the moment, happened to be uninterested and unwilling. We coax, wheedle, threaten, bribe. Reluctantly, he accepts our invitation. The game commences. And soon we notice that something is missing. Our reluctant partner goes through all the motions, he accepts the rules and follows them; he even appears *in a way* to have accepted the responsibilities of his role as a player. But something is missing. He is not "really playing." He is not playing for all its worth—indeed, it does not seem to be worth *anything* to him. He does not *care*. He is not concerned to win—or at least not concerned in the right way. His heart is not in it. He shows no sharp regret at losses; there is no triumph at wins; he can neither risk nor sacrifice, for the stakes are obviously of no value to him and hence their loss is no genuine risk, no genuine sacrifice. He does not, at decisive moments, brood, worry, think hard, then act either with conviction or fearful doubt. He never really wanted to play. The fact is, as we see by his not caring, he never really accepted our invitation to play in the spirit in which it was tendered. He is not really playing the game we want to play, but a formalistic parody of it. The game itself becomes pointless.

Not only the child and adult amateur, but the serious gambler, too, *cares.*

> Try giving him each morning the money he would be likely to win during the day. You will find he is anything but happy. One might say that what he wants is the pleasure of the game and not the winnings. Well, then, make him play for no stakes; he will find it devoid of interest, and will be bored.[4]

The gambler cares not about money but about winning the stakes in the way one is supposed to win them: in the spirit of the gamble, in conformity with the rules, and through the characteristic "action" of the game.

Serious game-players often speak of someone who *cares* in the spirit of the game as one who "plays a *responsible* game."

To care "in the spirit of the game" is very different from caring to play it. The spirit of the game (which includes following the rules) makes *its* demands upon us: our own pleasure, comfort, needs, tastes, or inclinations are to be ignored except insofar as they are allowed or required to come into play by the spirit of the game. The radical difference in the two uses of "care" is evident in the following: "As a matter of fact, I'd rather not play any more since I don't care for (enjoy) the game. But you can be mighty sure that if I do play, I'll play for all I'm worth; you needn't worry that I won't care! (i.e., devote all my efforts to playing in the spirit of the game—though I still will not enjoy it)."

It might seem that games are just the wrong thing to take as models for understanding moral responsibility; after all, we usually think of games as relaxation, a relaxation *from* our responsibilities. Is it possible that in using games or gambling as illustrations I have introduced a serious error? One may not care in playing tennis or bridge, but can one just not care to be morally responsible and in this way "get out of it"? Are there not certain moral responsibilities which are ours, certain things for which we must be held responsible whether we happen to care or not?

Should not an otherwise rational and healthy person be held responsible, whether he cares or not, for doing physical or mental injury to a person out of mere whim? And what if, on casual impulse, because he does not really care, he ignores family loyalty, fails to keep promises of great importance to others, betrays faith? Surely we hold—must hold—the individual morally responsible even if he does not care for the "game" or "in the spirit" of the "game." Morality is not a game! He *ought* to care; he should be *held* to it. . . .

Fluently, persuasively, the phrases come to mind, deeply tinged with feeling and arrayed in apparently seamless logic; our moral earnestness positively throbs as we contemplate—what? Are we now contemplating an actual or even a realistically imaginable situation of the relevant kind? Or is the moral engine idling here, turning, racing ever more furiously just because it is unimpeded by the friction of reality and the work-effort of actual use?

We must recall the real-life non-responsibles, either the full-blown psychopath or those with psychopathic ("irresponsible") tendencies. These individuals do typically evoke just such desperate outbursts of righteous intolerance, outbursts intended to be decisive, intended to cow, to shrivel evil pride, to fan the smoldering embers of decency. But, alas, those who must deal with such individuals, who face the exasperating, stupid, meaningless, exhaustingly repetitious—and withal casual—character of the genuinely non-responsible career must surrender. The surrender is not to a superior, evil resistance but to that which makes a mockery of our every effort: no resistance at all, no decency (or indecency, as such), no evil pride (no pride at all), no rebellion (and nothing cared for enough to spur rebellion).

If an individual will not play a game with us, we can still fall back on the intelligible framework of everyday life outside that game. But what if he will not enter life's fray itself in the spirit in which we enter it? To face such a person, such a reality (and not merely to think of it) is to experience a deep anxiety; a queasy helplessness moves in our soul.

Those who of necessity deal with such persons must come to terms with the truth and, as I have noted, radically change their approach. But those who can remain at a distance find it easier, usually, to mask their anxiety, even dissipate it, by the very intensity of their reaffirmed "moral indignation."

One would think that we ourselves had not compromised our own lives, refusing to accept responsibilities we might well accept, uncaring where we might well care, entirely willing to stand in righteous innocence because we would not, or think we could not, accept such further responsibilities. If acceptance and care are irrelevant, then we who are not hero-saints are all guilty. The irrelevance of acceptance implies a doctrine of original sin, universal guilt. This doctrine has a profound use, but I am at present concerned to establish just that perspective in which, it happens, the doctrine misguides. It obscures the kind of guilt, remorse, integrity, and the responsibility which are peculiar to those who have in some way accepted responsibility, who do care.

V

Until this point, I have made little distinction among such notions as "being a morally responsible person," "being morally responsible for an act already done," "being morally responsible for an act to be done," "being morally responsible for a range of possible acts," "being held responsible," "being assigned responsibility," "accepting responsibility," and so on. Nor have I clearly distinguished between "responsibility" and "moral responsibility," though for many purposes this, too, becomes important.

It is beyond the scope of this discussion to study in any detail either these distinctions or others one could make. I want to accomplish as briefly as possible one thing: to show that a large cluster of these, characteristically used in the moral life, has each of them a necessary dependence upon our judgment as to whether the individual is a morally responsible person. And a morally responsible person, in turn, is one who does accept responsibility, who shows the concern of responsibility. Thus my general thesis about the intimate interdependence of acceptance, care, and responsibility will be greatly extended in scope and, I hope, in depth.

We have already noted that the utterance of a responsibility-accepting formula is not a necessity. But now we must also remind ourselves that even if an individual does utter such a formula, this does not settle the question as to whether he has indeed accepted responsibility. One of the factors essential for the utterance to have force is that the individual be a responsible person. Obviously, a child, not being a responsible person, cannot accept responsibility for the welfare of a company of men, no matter how elaborately the ritualistic elements of assigning and accepting such "responsibility" may be carried through.

What is true in connection with the explicit utterance of formulae of acceptance is equally true of tacit acceptance. An individual who is insane cannot tacitly accept responsibility, nor can a child. Nor can we hold a person responsible for a specific act if he is not a responsible person at the time (though in psychotherapy he may later come to accept responsibility for it explicitly, having become in the meanwhile a responsible person).[5] Nor can we hold him responsible for a particular act which is yet to be done, nor assign him responsibility for an area of operations or of jurisdiction.

It is true that we may tell a psychotic person that he is "responsible" for keeping his room tidy, but if he does not do it, we merely shrug and adopt other measures. Of course, if he will do it, we will probably hold him to doing it—so long as he continues to do it. But our response to failure remains significantly different from what it is in the case of a responsible person. At most—and here we move to an important borderline of our categories—we may allow that he is a responsible person in some ways, and in those ways he is to be treated as such.

Here we can again take our clue from the raising of children. The child eventually becomes a responsible person by being treated more and more like one. But when he fails, we excuse him in saying: "he is only a child." As in the case of the psychotic, the more the child demonstrates a persistent, intelligent, and reasonably wide-ranging effectiveness and purposefulness in some area of his conduct, the more we are inclined to minimize the qualification in our treatment of him as a responsible person. When at last he comes to act consistently like a responsible person, then he *is* one, and only then.

It is, as always, the transitional phases which are of special interest and complexity for us. For example, we judge the normal eighteen-year-old to be fully responsible with regard to thievery or destruction of private property; but he is not yet fully responsible in the making of certain kinds of complex moral judgments, in the subtler discrimination of human relationships and feeling, in the sophisticated self-discipline of the appetites and emotions. At first he learns the more specific practices; he comes to care and—in this transitional sense—to accept "responsibility" in one or another special area of life. He is in some ways a responsible person. Then, with maturity, comes a more and more "generalized" responsibility as a *person.* Our language and comportment are peculiarly sensitive to context here: we may range from the one extreme of saying that only the saint is a fully responsible person to the other extreme of saying that even the child, the psychotic, the psychopath must be treated as responsible. But, as I have already indicated, the use of "responsibility" at either of these extremes differs decisively from its use in the mid-range of the more everyday adult world.

We are now in a position to see how an individual who has not even tacitly accepted responsibility in some particular matter or even in some specific range of conduct may yet be held responsible for it.

The man who walks by his neighbor's empty house and sees the driving rain pouring through a door blown open, who neither shuts the door himself nor bothers to mention it to the neighbor when he meets him in town—such a man is not legally responsible for the damage, but surely he had a moral responsibility in which he was remiss. If he claims, upon being censured, that he has never explicitly *or even tacitly* accepted responsibility for the keeping of his neighbor's house, we discount this. We do not reject his plea because acceptance of responsibility is unnecessary; nor do we discount his plea of non-responsibility because we think he really did, somehow, tacitly accept that specific responsibility. No, we take the stand we do because he is a responsible *person.*

In accepting responsibility as a responsible *person,* we tacitly engage ourselves to take on a vast, and antecedently unspecifiable, range of specific responsibilities. The responsible person is one who has learned to identify a reasonable variety of these when he comes upon them. And he distinguishes these cases where he is antecedently committed from those very many cases where he is antecedently uncommitted. He knows the ropes, though there is no rule book.

"He knows the ropes." Or does he? Not always, not infallibly. He may cry, "I never took responsibility for my neighbor's house!"—and then *we* must call himself to himself, to the responsibilities he has accepted as a responsible person. "You *should* have!" we reply. But the path along which we track down tacit acceptance leads rapidly into the densest of woods. The dappled lights and darks which camouflage the past, the tangle of memories entwined with fantasies, all can lead us into the black caves. The miracle is not that we do get lost at times but that we so frequently do not.

If there is at all any moral *life* in a person and not merely moral routine, then a significant part of that life consists in *coming to learn* the scope of the responsibility which he has already accepted. There is nothing self-evidently wrong about the notion of *learning* what it is that we have already accepted. Parallels are plentiful. We learn from logical operations the unsuspected implications of our axioms; by experience and by legal analysis we may learn much later that the contract we signed makes us responsible in unsuspected ways. As in the case of moral responsibility, so in the case of law: there is no clear line between not realizing what one has genuinely contracted to do, and not being under contract at all just because one was so ignorant of the possible import of what one was doing. In morals there is no earthly judge to enforce or to annul the contract. And, unfortunately, the mind's eye has a tropism, turning instinctively to gaze on the glitter of possible profit and away from the shadows of actual cost.

Just what moral responsibility have I accepted in presenting myself as a responsible person? I may upon occasion be shattered to discover the answer, yet admit that it is correct. I may need to be called to account by others: we use argument, persuasion, pedagogical threats, name-calling—the devices and the methods are innumerable, depending upon the nature of the case. In quite different ways, preaching, moral argument and appeal, psychotherapy, sanctions, and rewards all play their role at times.

Yet we must not forget that all of this must end, and it does so in that region which is at the "extreme limit" of *morality* as well as of moral inquiry. For to appeal at all, we must always, finally, appeal to some acknowledged responsibility, perhaps tacitly accepted, but in any case some responsibility which the individual does accept, something for which, and in the spirit of which, he cares. Ultimately, we make this deepest and broadest appeal to the person as a responsible person—then we must wait.

Am I the keeper of my neighbor's house? Am I my brother's keeper? Is this what I have accepted in taking on the role of the responsible person?

God says "Yes" to Cain, and condemns him to live. The history of man until now would tell us "No." The Grand Inquisitor, speaking for history, says that men *will* not accept such burdensome responsibility; hence they are, in godly eyes, non-responsible. The Inquisitor therefore sees Man as the child who *will* not grow up, as the psychopath; the Christ sees man as the child, and children will grow up. There is nothing to argue here. The Inquisitor receives no rebuttal, only a gesture. For us poor mortals, in the limbo between history and God, it is our own gesture, at this extreme limit, which decides.

NOTES

1. Immanuel Kant, *Foundations of the Metaphysics of Morals,* trans. by L. W. Beck (Chicago: University of Chicago Press, 1950), Section III.

2. Gilbert Ryle, "On Forgetting the Difference Between Right and Wrong," in A. Melden, *Essays in Moral Philosophy* (Seattle: University of Washington Press, 1958), p. 156.

3. Hervey Clegley, *The Mask of Sanity,* 2nd ed. (St. Louis: C. V. Mosby & Co., 1950), esp. pp. 357–379.

4. Blaise Pascal, *Pensées,* trans. by H. F. Stewart (New York: Pantheon Books, 1950), p. 63.

5. Herbert Fingarette, *The Self in Transformation* (New York: Basic Books, 1963), Ch. 4.

3 / Self-Insight as Self-Discovery, Self-Realization, Self-Creation

I

In contemporary psychotherapeutic theory, there are three contrasting, and, in a sense, competing concepts: (1) the (Freudian) notion of *self-discovery,* (2) the (Existentialist) notion of *self-creation,* and (3) the (Aristotelian) notion of *self-realization.*

The argument over these different ways of conceptualizing therapeutic self-transformation has usually been carried on by individuals already committed to one or another viewpoint. Naturally, a writer takes his own conceptual scheme as the correct one, and then shows how he can account for an opponent's data in his own presumably more adequate language. Useful as this technique of argument is for some purposes, it obscures certain issues which a more neutral language might exhibit clearly.

Such a language—for I do think there is one which will serve the present purpose—is the language of everyday human intercourse. It is the language of human beings *as* human, of persons encountering one another *as* persons. It is, as we shall see, the language in which psychotherapeutic understanding has deep roots.

It is the first objective of this study to provide an outline of the nature of psychotherapeutic insight, and to do so entirely in this everyday language of human intercourse. This account will then be used to throw light upon those features of therapeutic self-transformation which suggest one or another of the three different technical conceptual schemes mentioned. It is not my aim to produce still a new, fourth doctrine of psychotherapy. My aim is, rather, to provide fresh insight into the already familiar technical doctrines, and also into the nature of self-transformation.

Implicit, but also important, in this study is the perspective of recent philosophical analysis in England and America. This renewed philosophical interest in psychology is, so far as I know, almost entirely unrepresented in the professional psychological literature. Though strikingly different in style and import, it has important historical and logical relations with logical positivism. As we know, the latter once dominated philosophy and still remains gospel among large numbers of experimentally and scientifically oriented students of human conduct. A new philosophical insight of one generation often does become an influential methodological doctrine for the psychologists of the next generation. (And movement in the reverse direction is equally common.) It may be, then, that this newer philosophical approach is destined to foreshadow some forthcoming phases of development of methodology in the empirical study of man. It is of special relevance to those concerned with clarity and rigor in the development of a genuinely humanistic psychology.

II

There is a distinctive feature of dynamic psychotherapy which I wish at once to emphasize: in the therapeutic contact itself, therapist and patient deal with the patient's problem in ordinary, human terms. "Ordinary, human terms" is a vague phrase, but it can be quickly and adequately clarified for our purposes. The language and techniques of insight therapy contrast sharply, for example, with those of electrical, physical, or chemical therapy. The rationale and method of the latter forms of treatment can be adequately formulated only in terms of esoteric technical terms drawn from the various physical and life sciences. These are terms and techniques which are essentially foreign to the everyday actions and concerns of the layman. The dynamic therapist, on the other hand, whatever his technical background theory, uses the *patient's* language when he works with the patient. This is the language of ordinary human action and passion: "I hate," "You want," "I dreamed," "My reason was," "She told me," and so on. The therapist, in his moments of reflection, may conceive of certain conduct, as, for example, a reaction-formation used as defense against unconscious aggression. But in his direct psychotherapeutic dealing with the patient, he may merely say, "Hm," or interpose a gently skeptical "You do?" when the patient embroiders upon the theme that he has vast and unqualified respect for his father. With a more literate patient, the everyday idiom may be flavored with phrases or allusions familiar to the cultivated person: perhaps an allusion to "protesting too much," perhaps even the Shakespearean quotation itself. Or the therapist may eventually feel it appropriate to speak much more explicitly and directly: "Your constant worrying about your father's dying was really a kind of disguised daydream that he *would* die and leave you free of his domination, wasn't it?" Such means, whether cryptic or explicit, extend insight into new areas of our experience, but they consist of the language and gesture of everyday human intercourse. The therapeutic dialogue proper moves without recourse to esoteric theory or technical instruments.

I am going to start from this thesis that all dynamic psychotherapies do their actual work within the perspective of human intercourse. Therefore, instead of describing therapeutic self-transformation in terms of hypothetical causal mechanisms, whether psychic structures or physiochemical processes, or instead of employing a metaphysical language based upon Being, Existence, Potentialities, or a True Self, I am going to talk about the situation as one in which two human beings engage in an exploration of the sufferings which one of them is undergoing.

The terms I use will, as a consequence, be so familiar and unsophisticated-looking by comparison to our usual technical terminologies as to be deceptive. The impulse to flee the everyday language and everyday truths of human experience and to seek a special intellectual comfort in the use of a technical language is an impulse we must fight throughout this analysis. It is not that technical languages are unnecessary. However, for the present purpose, we must exhibit the facts in a non-technical language in order later to throw light upon the sources and character of the technical languages.

Let us begin, then, by supposing a very common sort of neurotic conflict. A college student pursuing a premedical career is unable to get down to work and do his assignments. There are no physical obstacles or social restraints. He is disturbed, puzzled. We ask him informally for further information. His father is a physician. The father had suggested that he could be of aid to the son in later years, should the son follow in his footsteps. The son has no particular interest in medicine, loves to read books in such "impractical" areas as history and related fields, but agrees that his father's suggestion is indeed both sensible and benevolent. His father, in this matter as in most, has shown great concern for the son's welfare and has carefully guided him. The student feels unreserved appreciation for this. But he is all the more concerned about his inability to settle down to his pre-medical studies.

We could, in very general terms, analyze this common sort of situation as one in which "aggressive impulses evoke anxiety" which in turn arouses "defenses leading to repression" and to the observed symptoms as a "disguised return of the repressed aggression." Or we could view the situation in terms of "alienation from the true self," frustration of the "primary potentialities," a failure of "self-realization." Or, again, we might see it as an "evasion of authentic choice," a refusal to face "existential anxiety," and we might refer, perhaps, to his mode of "being-in-the-world."

Naturally, each of the preceding formulations is not intended to be a precise diagnosis but simply a reminder of a general conceptual framework within which a precise diagnosis might be formulated. It is our purpose here, however, to provide a non-technical description of what we see. What is this non-technical description?

It must be stated in terms of features of the situation which are obvious to any reasonably observant layman. I shall first state summarily and roughly what these features are, and then I shall elaborate on them.

It is obvious that the student has some reasons for pursuing a medical career (e.g., fatherly advice, the hope of substantial rewards, and so on). He also has reasons for *not* wanting to pursue a medical career (e.g., lack of interest in the subject matter). And, further, he has reasons (e.g., loyalty, affection for father) for wanting not to acknowledge, even to himself, that he does not want or that there is even any reason not to want a medical career.

We notice more still: though he has reason for acting in a variety of (conflicting) ways, he is not in any *normal* way acting in any of these ways. Nevertheless, we notice aspects of his behavior which are highly suggestive of each of these ways. Much of what he does is *like* what one would do if one were studying medicine—but, of course, an essential element is missing: he doesn't study. Also, what he is doing is very much like what one would do if one were sulking or rebelling against the demand that one study medicine. But, once again, a number of the typical essentials of what we *normally* call rebellion are missing: on many occasions he either does not speak appropriately, or he does not express appropriate feelings, or he does not act appropriately. For example, he is sincerely horrified at the suggestion that he is rebelling; he sincerely denies it. And a *sincere* denial that one is doing something is not normally an element in the doing of it. There is, finally, much in his behavior that suggests what one would do if one were *hiding* rebelliousness—but many of the words and deeds of the normal act of keeping a secret are missing. This is not a straightforward case of "just pretending" that he wants to cooperate and do his work.

Now, I believe that this first sketchy analysis of the situation reports the essential outlines of what any perceptive person could and often does notice. To say it all takes time; but once we have talked to the student or read the original précis of his case history, to notice it all takes but a moment. To notice it requires no technical language, no special insight into secret inner processes or metaphysical truths. The things I have pointed out are, individually, just the sorts of everyday, open-to-observation details which human beings are constantly noticing as they appraise one another in daily intercourse. My analysis may seem, for that very reason, to remain on the surface—and indeed that is my aim. Whether this is "superficial" is another question. It is the question whether profundity in these matters consists only in going "below the surface" to unobservables, or whether it may also consist in properly apprehending what is already open to observation.

It will be advisable at this point to digress for a few paragraphs in order to clarify and justify my use of terms like "reason" and "normal"—two terms likely to provoke uneasiness in the social or psychological scientist's mind. Yet they are essential if we are to grasp the meaning of what we observe and what we infer.

Obviously, if we had no sense of what is normal, i.e., appropriate or fitting in this situation, we would have no basis in the first place for suspecting neurosis or irrationality in the student's behavior. It is only because we agree on the appropriateness of certain acts, given certain motives and situations, that we notice at once the inappropriateness, the abnormality of the student's not studying. Our agreement on what is normal may be buttressed by careful analysis and justification, but it need not be. It may be an uncritical tacit agreement. Or it may be that "normal" in this context must remain an undefined term in any theory of psychotherapy. In any case, it is of the essence to see that our inferences from observable behavior to hidden motives, or "true selves," or "world-designs" are inevitably based upon our taking for granted the appropriateness of certain conduct to those hidden sources. We ask, for example: of what motive would persistently-not-studying be an appropriate expression? At once there pops into anyone's mind as a live and obvious possibility: he doesn't *want* to study—*that* would be an appropriate motive for *not* studying. Since not wanting to study is a motive of which not studying would be a fitting expression, we may tentatively postulate that this is in fact the motive. The very obviousness of this relationship is what enables us to "see" at once the plausibility of many a psychiatric "interpretation." What confuses is the student's initial assertion that he does want to study.

The psychiatric inference, then, begins with the assumption that we agree, in some instances at least, upon what acts are *normal* expressions of what motives. Dynamic explanations are plausible because they state an *appropriate* motive for what had seemed pointless behavior. If we did not already agree in some way on what is appropriate, there would be no sense of illumination when an unsuspected motive is suggested as the "true" one.

The next step in psychiatric inference also may be put in everyday terms. It involves asking the question: What are the *reasons* which make certain motives appropriate? If you find something which is *normally* a reason for having a certain motive, then, other things being equal, you can suppose the motive to be present. We *understand* a person's having a motive when we are shown that he has reason for having that motive. Is there anything which would normally be a reason for the student's not *wanting* to study (a motive we now tentatively suppose to be present)? Yes, he has what we ordinarily do consider reasons to rebel against his father's advice and to refuse to study medicine. To mention only one such reason, he does not like studying biology and he likes studying history. It is only when we see that he has *reasons* to rebel that we feel light has been thrown on his *wanting* to rebel. Thus, in summary, we detect *reasons for* not wanting to study medicine, and we see behavior which, though eccentric, strongly suggests conduct which would normally *flow from* the motive of not wanting to study. The supposition that this *is* one of his motives takes on explanatory value under these conditions. But notice: each step requires that we already agree on what is a normal reason for and an expression of certain motives. Here we are at the axiomatic foundations of psychiatric understanding.

It was Freud's insight that the psychoneurotic has *reasons* for what he does: i.e., motives for his acts, and reasons for his motives. This is by no means to say that the psychoneurotic's conduct is the wisest or best *on the whole*. We merely postulate that he has *some* reason for it: i.e., that there is something in the light of which, other things being equal, his motive or conduct would be appropriate.

Let us apply the preceding comments on "normal" and "reason" to an analysis of the student's denial that he is rebelling. Here, too, we try to understand his behavior according to the same principles of inference. It is obvious, i.e., tacitly agreed, that a denial of rebellion by one who (we now suppose) is in fact rebellious is a normal expression of the wish to hide rebellion. And the reasons for having such a wish are normally such things as fear of punishment or loss of love. Since such reasons exist here, and since the behavior is appropriate to the wish to hide rebellion, we tentatively suppose the existence of such a motive.

In this discussion of the role of "normal" and "reason," I have over-simplified a crucial aspect of the matter to which we shall very shortly return. But, before we leave explicit discussion of "normal," one further brief comment may be advisable.

Normal, as we use it here, does not imply "conformist" or socially "adaptive." Nor is it a statistical concept. What is appropriate in a new situation may come as a surprise, may be utterly novel, and yet, once considered, be recognized as precisely what was appropriate. It is clear that the artist is one who, in his work, finds precisely what is appropriate; yet it is always novel in some way. The "conformist" is a parody of this: he equates appropriateness with strict obedience to a command or with the rigid following of some fixed rule. But as we know—don't ask me how we know it, but it is, in any case, an essential axiom of therapy—following a rule rigidly can be inappropriate in many a situation in life. "Appropriate" or "normal" in this normative sense are essential notions in psychological understanding. It is my object here to exhibit and develop the import of such axiomatic notions in the context of psychiatric use, not to justify them in any direct way.

We now return to the description in everyday language of the student's behavior, and now we must consider an important qualification of the over-simple analysis presented. I return to a thesis stated in the original summary account of the student's conflict.

In no case, whether in regard to his obeying his father, rebelling, or hiding his rebellion, is the student doing *precisely* what is normal. His actions are not normal studying or normal rebellion, and, hence, they are not, *strictly* speaking, appropriate to the motives we have tentatively postulated. His conduct is abortive, fragmented, and incomplete, however we try to classify it. It is not only that we notice important elements or aspects of normal obedience, normal rebellion, or normal secrecy are missing. Equally noticeable is the fact that, whichever course of conduct we take as basis for analysis, there is a lack of self-control, a loss of self-directedness at crucial points. From the standpoint of this very general but important criterion of self-control, we cannot say in any normal sense that the student is studying, or rebelling, or hiding his motives. For each of these is characteristically a course of *conduct,* i.e., a voluntary and self-directed course of action. Because of the lack of intelligent self-control, and because of the fragmented nature of his behavior, we see all this as *pathology* rather than as a normal but complex set of motives such as we find in our everyday actions.

We are now in a position to see *why* it is that the student cannot control his behavior at crucial points. Just because he is not involved in any normal course of conduct, his behavior is to him unintelligible. His own conception of his conduct certainly does not fit his behavior. Guiding himself by it, he becomes puzzled and helpless at crucial points. Indeed, his conduct, as it stands, is *objectively* unintelligible; strictly speaking, it is behavior but not conduct. There are isolated fragments, bits and pieces of behavior which, in other contexts, *could be* elements in some course of conduct or other. It is like a Lewis Carroll nonsense poem: the elements, even portions of the structure, are familiar, but the specific combinations don't make genuine sense. It is frustratingly familiar, and we feel we ought to seize the meaning; but at crucial points we find ourselves baffled.

No wonder the neurotic loses control over his behavior, though he feels he *ought* to be able to control it. Though it looks deceptively like conduct, in fact conduct has broken down; he is disorganized. He can't *make* anything of what he is doing: because he can't make it out, he can't make it into anything.

If the reader is tempted at this point to argue that the student's conduct may not be *normal* rebellion but is unconscious or abnormal rebellion, let the reader beware. This way of putting the matter begs the very question I wish to examine. For the introduction of such technical conceptions as "unconscious rebellion" is precisely a way of emphasizing that the conduct is *not* normal rebellion. Calling it unconscious rebellion at this stage of our argument is merely a way of emphasizing that it may profitably be thought of *in connection* with rebellious conduct because the usual reasons for rebellion are there and because some of the typical marks of rebellious attitude and behavior are present. But I have already pointed all this out without recourse to the technical term "unconscious." The same considerations apply to the proposal that we adopt the label "abnormal" rebellion. In short, I am trying to bring out explicitly the complex but familiar sorts of detailed observations which psychotherapists ordinarily wrap into a package and label with a technical term such as "unconscious." But it is these key technical terms which I want later to examine in the light of a reasonably full non-technical account. I shall continue, then, to emphasize the everyday description of the facts and refrain from jumping to the use of technical terms as short cuts.

It is clear that what the student needs if he is to regain self-control is some way to get back on the track of doing something intelligible; he needs to engage in a definite course of conduct, however complexly motivated, a course of conduct which is appropriate to his circumstances. This need provides us with our major clues to the aims of insight therapy. And we are now prepared to sketch the main features of therapy which bear directly upon the generation of what is often called dynamic insight.

The therapist encourages the patient (our college student) to talk about himself, his life, his world. And we must turn at once to those phases of therapy where the therapist is prepared to make gestures or comments of a therapeutic sort. It is not relevant to our analysis here what specific theoretical orientation the therapist has, provided he aims at insight. We are here primarily interested in certain practices ubiquitous in insight therapy.

The therapist, in his interventions, does not operate by formula or direct theoretical deduction. In the therapeutic situation, he uses intuition. But what is it to use intuition? Is it a special kind of esoteric act, a special form of mental grasping? Here, too, we must go behind the word and consider, in the language of human conduct, what happens. Let us put aside theoretical presuppositions. The therapist does not set himself to perform some esoteric act of mental apprehension. He listens and observes, and he responds (though often silently) to the situation. It is no more esoteric than, for example, the following: I enter a room; there are several persons present. One comes up to me, extends his hand, and introduces himself. I do not have to *think* about custom, courtesy obligations, or what have you. What I see calls forth from me spontaneously the proper response—not a conditioned reflex but an intelligent though unself-conscious response. I have already learned how to respond intelligently in this sort of situation. Such a response need not, and ordinarily does not, include going through an inner dialogue or intellectual inquiry in order to discover what to do. To act intelligently in this situation is simply to offer my hand, to do it without having to "figure it out," and to do it properly. How this comes about may, in a number of respects, be a mystery. But the fact is familiar, and the average person learns to do it, as a result of familiar sorts of training, but without any need to know the physics or neurology of it. We are not denying that there are complex problems for many a scientist here when we take note that there is no problem for our particular inquiry. We need only note that psychotherapy starts from the assumption that people do learn how to act intelligently and spontaneously, though not uniformly well in all situations.

So the therapist is like the man who, in a relaxed and natural setting, enters the room and responds to greetings and to the gestures of those who welcome him. The therapist, more specifically, listens and observes—not as a detached scientist, but as one who is ready to respond as soon as there is even a quasi-intelligible gesture to respond to. Perhaps the therapist's distinctive skill is that he has cultivated the patience to remain "open" to the situation even when it does not call forth immediately some clear response. Most of us can't bear being puzzled about what's going on—if no spontaneous response occurs, we become anxious and we start *thinking* about what to do. But the therapist *can* bear just waiting.

Characteristically, the therapist is open to the totality

of the patient's gesture; he is not so dominated as the layman by the avowals of the patient whenever those avowals don't really "fit" into the total situation. The therapist has learned to respond sensitively to irrationalities, inappropriatenesses, conduct which is not in all its aspects—speech, tone, affect, body gesture, formal consistency—"of a piece." In everyday life we tend to overlook these things in order not to confuse ourselves intellectually and emotionally.

Perhaps the therapist feels as if he were under attack. But the words which the patient uses are normally used as friendly words. The therapist, unimpressed by this, pays serious attention to his own spontaneous response. *Something* about the conduct of this person brings out in the therapist the response characteristic of being a target of an aggressive, rebellious attack.

The therapist has learned to allow his own response to emerge more fully, more recognizably to his own inspection, but yet covertly and with limited intensity. He pays attention to the patient's behavior when this response is "triggered." In this way, by allowing segments of the patient's behavior to cue a response of a normal kind in the therapist, the latter discovers the normal response *most nearly suggested* by the patient's abnormal behavior. The more his response is sensitively appropriate to the patient's behavior rather than stereotyped or initiated by the therapist's own private needs, the more honestly and accurately the therapist can identify his own response when it emerges, the more sensitively he can control that response by limiting its intensity and overt expression, and the more he will succeed in tactfully focusing his own and the patient's attention upon the latter's role in evoking that response.

For example: Suppose that at some point the therapist, sufficiently "attuned" to the patient's doings, senses that the patient's reasons for being ashamed, afraid, or guilty about rebelliousness are no longer overwhelmingly strong. He may then intuitively act upon the opportunity. He may point out to the patient—in the very moment of the patient's desperate cries about wishing to get on with his studies—that the patient also has reasons for *not* wanting to study. Or he may emphasize that some feature of the patient's behavior is suggestive of his *not* wanting to study.

In effect, though not in so many words perhaps, the therapist says: "You say you want to study medicine, but you do not study. This fact is strange if you do want to study, but it is absolutely consistent with your not wanting to study. Now what is more, you do have reasons, though you never mention them as such, for not wanting to study: you admittedly have no interest in the subject matter itself!"

In pointing this out, he may lead the student for the first time to pay attention to this lack of interest, to allow himself to *feel its force as a reason* for not wanting to study. "That's true, I'm not exactly interested in biology.

In fact . . . you know . . . funny I never thought of it this way . . . I've done good work in biology a few times . . . but I was bored by it. In fact—gosh, I was *so* bored . . ." and so on.

If the moment was well chosen, the student will accept the invitation to dwell on his reasons; he will be, for the first time, engaged in the first gestures of the course of conduct which follows naturally from those reasons, a course of conduct which is in other contexts perfectly familiar to him. In a rapid but natural manner, the student *becomes* resentful (in the normal sense) at having to study biology. For the first time he will not become panicky at this spontaneous and naturally developing course of conduct. This is because the therapist has done his job (we presume) and has been tactful and effective in familiar ways which we cannot digress to mention here; therefore the student will so perceive his situation that he will not have reason to become panicky. He will feel assured that at this particular moment there are no reasons for unbearable fear, guilt, or shame. The student soon bursts out with open, perhaps violent words, feeling, gestures—but they will all be appropriate to each other and to the reasons whose force he has at last acknowledged. It will be normal rebellion against studying rather than involuntary and unintelligible breakdown in studying.

Now that he is doing something intelligible and familiar, now that he is engaged in a definite course of conduct emerging intelligibly out of one situation and leading intelligibly toward another, the student is self-controlled. This should not be confused with the supposition that he is self-consciously planning, "controlling" his every word and deed. It is the kind of self-control a skilled bicycle rider has as distinguished from the lack of control of a beginner. What the patient does is complex, spontaneous, and no doubt not exactly like anything he has ever done before. But that is the case with all intelligent action, for, although it is appropriate, it is never merely repetitive.

We may compare the neurotic to one who walks in a trick room: he thinks he is walking upward, but at every step he loses self-control because the floor really slopes downward. In this room, every attempt to correct himself in terms of his own interpretation of the situation puts him again at the mercy of forces beyond his control. In such a situation if he can only find some course of action which he knows how to perform intelligently and which also is appropriate, he will regain self-control. "Close your eyes; slide your feet on the floor, and then keep going." These are things he *can* do. And in this particular situation they will work. "Consider your reasons for *not* wanting to study—and go on from there." *Now* the student finds himself doing and saying things which cohere; they make sense and he can do them sensibly.

Of course, if there is nothing appropriate which the

person has learned to do, he will have to learn for the first time. The landsman has to learn to swim for the first time. Though he begins by doing things he already can do ("revolve your arms like a windmill; kick your legs as if they were a scissors"), he eventually develops a smoother and quite unique kind of conduct which is skilled swimming. Analogously, if the patient in therapy has had very restricted opportunities in some area of life, he may have to learn for the first time, in therapy, how to act in certain ways. The college student may have been so restricted in regard to expressing resentment that he must have time to be *educated,* by practice, in moving from infantile rage to adult anger. In such cases, as we know, premature interpretations by the therapist may release uncontrollable impulses, i.e., *uncivilized* responses. Therapy often requires a certain amount of education as a preliminary to insight. Insight therapy relies upon the maturity of the patient; it is aimed at relatively isolated immaturities.

I hardly need note here that there are many complexities in therapy which I have not touched upon. Even at this length, I have only been able to sketch the merest outline of a way of seeing therapy within the framework of the everyday language of human intercourse.

III

Now we turn directly to the three approaches to psychotherapy mentioned at the outset of this study: therapy as a discovery of the unconscious self, as creation of a new self, and as realization of a potential self. First let us ask: In what way is therapy the discovery of an unconscious self?

Of course there is much in therapy which consists, in a very obvious sense, of the discovery or recall of truths about oneself and one's past. The patient may recall a forgotten childhood event and then ask eyewitnesses, if still available, for further information. More startling, however, is a different sort of discovery. In taking up some feature of his life, and in elaborating upon it normally for the first time, the patient does not realize beforehand what is to come. He is often surprised at what he finds himself doing and at the outcome. He is responding spontaneously to the immediate situation, and this means he is not thinking about it beforehand, not trying to predict or plan the outcome. It is a truism that therapy thrives on the direct and spontaneous (intuitive) response of the patient, whereas therapy is blocked when all responses are delayed out of concern for the ultimate results. When we observe something which we had not known or expected beforehand, we quite properly turn to the language of discovery.

Thus the patient *discovers* feelings, thoughts, and actions emerging. They *come* to him. Yet, although his conduct is both surprising and unpredicted, it is nevertheless reasonable, appropriate, self-controlled. Thus he discovers himself acting as we all do when we are most at one with ourselves and the world, most at ease. At such moments we do not *plan* our thoughts and feelings ahead of time: we *have* them at the appropriate moment. And we feel them to be ours. Since they do not come in isolation but from an intelligible context in which they are appropriate, they do not have the alien character of the obsessive or hallucinatory thought, word, or deed. What happens may be utterly novel or utterly routine, but it is *à propos*. This is the kind of discovery which goes with intelligent spontaneity, with freedom and autonomy, not with self-alienation or depersonalization.

Because of this sense of discovery and the specific form of "passivity" which in its own special way such discovery requires, it is plausible to develop a therapeutic theory centering around the notion of discovery. And the language of discovery is the language of the exposure of what was hidden and is now at last exposed. We speak of discovering what Freud called the unconscious where there were reasons for a response, and usually where there are recognizable elements of that response, but where there is also a systematic inability to allow the natural response to emerge normally and *in toto*, to emerge with appropriate language, gesture, and feeling in relation to the context. When the response at last does emerge normally, it is "discovered." This "discovery" language suggests—and the other facts encourage us to modify ordinary usage and say that (in a new and special sense) the response "was there already" but is only discovered now. We tag this peculiar usage by adding the label "unconscious" to motives when we assert that they have been, in this special sense, "already there."

I have tried in the immediately preceding to bring out the features of the situation which lend themselves to the use of the language of discovery, with its attendant theoretical and practical elaboration. But there are also features of the therapeutic transformation which entitle us to use the language of choice, decision, and of self-creation with its attendant anxiety. We must now turn our attention to these aspects of the matter.

At various times during therapy the patient must be ready to forgo, at least for the moment, his own insistent version of the meaning of his conduct. He has reasons for insisting, for example, that he is wholeheartedly in sympathy with his father's advice. He has reasons for avoiding alternative accounts of his conduct—especially the alternative of rebellion, an alternative very likely to be suggested. But if therapy is proceeding successfully, these reasons for insisting on his former account of affairs either disappear or are perceived in a fresh way which reduces their force. The time comes when the patient senses that the giving up of his old view and way of acting is a serious and immediate possibility. He is as yet, as I have noted, unclear as to where a new course of conduct would lead. Nor will he really discover this until he enters upon it and finds out. Thus there is inherent in therapy what Kiors [1] calls the "existential moment in psychotherapy," the moment when one faces the future as unforeseeable. This acceptance is, of course, not mere intellectual assent; it is an *experience*. It is to face anxiety. Then the patient, either quickly or slowly, does begin to sense dimly the outlines of the new options, though their full character and "feel" are still unclear to him.

The student, trembling inwardly, decides that he will present his case against studying medicine to his father. He arranges to speak with him alone, forces himself to marshal his arguments, to be reasonable and forceful. Suddenly, in the midst of the interview he finds himself becoming bolder, less rigidly and self-consciously "reasonable," more spontaneously self-assertive. He hears himself announcing in a tone he has never used before, a tone spontaneously unlike his usual high-pitched and cautious one, "Damn it, Dad, medicine just isn't for me!" He talks as man to man. And the world does not shatter about him.

Therapy, then, takes courage. It does literally involve acting and thinking and feeling in *new* ways. And not all of this is "discovery." Although the larger outcome of the patient's change is neither planable nor foreseeable, there are many essential intermediate steps which, in a quite ordinary sense, call for what is, on crucial occasions, courageous decision or choice. For it is only by making day-to-day decisions and by summoning up his courage and sensibilities that he can expose himself to novel transformative situations. If he can arrange, or at least "stay with," such situations, he can cultivate root, trunk, and branch of that new conduct whose seed was sown in the moment of response to the therapist's gesture. Thus it is that the language of decision, of choice, and consequently of self-creation has its use. The patient was not—in the ordinary or "literal" sense—rebellious before: he has had the courage and the wit to do the things and expose himself to the situation which, for the first time, allow him to *become* rebellious. Becoming rebellious, and discovering that he is, he then has the courage to accept what he has become; he does not fight against it or deny it. He is a "new man."

In the case of the preceding illustration, we would naturally turn to the language of discovery if we emphasize the sudden, the unexpected, the unplanned but appropriate performance at the last of the interview with his father. If, however, we emphasize his deliberate arrangements to speak to his father and to express his opposition, the considering, weighing, adopting, and sticking with a course of conduct, then the language of decision seems natural to use. But now suppose that we take still a third view of the situation. We shall see that there are the usual conditions which permit the use of the language of potentiality.

Although what the student feels, says, and does now is new, it incorporates, after all, fragments of his former behavior. These fragments are now elements in intelligible conduct. Furthermore, this conduct is tied to the very reasons which had functioned abortively in the past, reasons upon which he had never acted appropriately until now. From this angle we are impressed by the continuity in the midst of change. More than this, we see a continuity leading from an abortive and fragmented past to a present in which what was abortive is now brought to birth, what was fragmented is now intelligibly integrated. Or, to put the matter less metaphorically, old behavior, formerly pathological and meaningless, is now integrated into conduct which has intelligible origins in the past, continuity in the present, and dependable consummation in the future. Hence, we find it natural, from *this* perspective, to speak of "making real," real-izing, that which much earlier did not exist but already had reason to be. By engaging in some appropriate course of conduct—however unusual in a statistical sense it may be, or however unpopular—the patient is making real the self which there had long been reason to make real. He is realizing his "*true*" potentiality, i.e., the potentiality for a reasonable self, not merely any potentiality. The teleology of potentiality is admissible here because we are concerned not with the past as physical cause but with the past as it embodied *reasons* for action. Such an emphasis brings us more sympathetically to a language of self-transformation such as Fromm, for example, uses. Fromm says: "Man's main task in life is to give birth to himself, to become what he potentially is." [2]

We need now to consider one last perspective on therapeutic insight, a perspective which reveals much about the three ways we have used to characterize self-transformation. This last perspective reveals the peculiar role of the past in establishing a personal identity.

The patient, after insight, sees his own past in a new way. He cannot help seeing it in the light of the intelligible forms of conduct to which he now has assimilated, *retrospectively*, all his behavior. This implies that he would now write a significantly different autobiography from what he would have written before therapy. Our student, for example, might now say about his past: "I wouldn't give in to my father, though I was afraid to defy him openly." This is a far cry from what he would have said about this same period of life in the absence of therapy, e.g.: "I tried to be honestly cooperative with my father, for I have always believed his advice has been wise and well meant."

Now, one's personal history as grasped by oneself is perhaps the single most important element in one's own sense of personal identity. The physical identity of the body does not of itself suffice to provide one's sense of *personal* identity. The amnesiac, as we know, sees the same physical body he has always seen, but this of itself does not establish his personal identity to himself. As a person, he is a stranger to himself. He does not recognize the person by looking at the body. Indeed, even if one could, by means of photos and documents, show him that his is the same body which someone named John Jones had, he does not recognize himself as John Jones —except as an "object," or for purposes of legal identity. In his own consciousness, John Jones is a stranger. His sense of *personal* identity is rooted in his sense of his past. If he does not feel himself to have a past, he does not feel himself to have an identity. It follows that to change his sense of his past is to change his personal identity in his own eyes—though it is not to change his legal or social identity, of course. In psychotherapy, a person who achieves insight may well be changing his sense of the past, and, according to this criterion, he is a different person.

Some analogues may help us here. The judge by his *present* decision provides the legal *past* with an authoritative characterization; and in doing this he also redirects the future course of affairs. The referee by his *present decision* authoritatively assigns to what has happened its intelligible place in the scheme of *past* happenings ("It *was* a knockout," the referee *now* pronounces). The student, in accepting now the force of certain reasons, acknowledges their force in similar situations in the past as well. Thus the patient authoritatively reinterprets his past. This is his personal sense of the past; it is the past which provides his sense of personal identity.

If he has been inclined to use the language of self-discovery in therapy, he will be inclined to speak of discovering his *true* past. This will in turn suggest a theory of hidden processes, objects, or events: Freudian metapsychology and the unconscious. If, however, he has been inclined to think of therapy as essentially self-creation, he will be encouraged to speak of this change of the past as a reconstruction of the self, a peculiarly radical self-re-creation, since it involves the past and future self as well as the present self. But how can one speak of now changing the past? The paradox this produces in relation to our language of time and reality will encourage the development of a metaphysical language involving such notions as the "transcendence of time" and different "orders of reality."

Finally, we may expect one who is already inclined to the language of self-realization to follow through the complications, knowingly or unknowingly, in the language of Aristotelian metaphysics. For the notion of teleological development implicit in the language of "potentiality" makes a language of mere past causality ("efficient" causality) uncongenial. And, on the other hand, the emphasis on the continuity of past and future makes the language of radical novelty, of "creation," equally uncongenial. It is not that those who speak of self-realization have based their views on Aristotle; rather it is that Aristotle elaborated systematically and clearly the pattern of language to which a person is committed if he consistently applies the notion of potentiality in a teleological sense.

It is well for us to explore intensively each of these aspects of the therapeutic experience, and it is natural and effective to use the language which fits that aspect best. Need we suppose that one perspective is *the* most correct or profound? There are an indefinite number of ways of talking about the same event; the important question is: which ones are profitable or illuminating, and under what sorts of circumstances and for what investigative purposes are they so? All this cannot be decided *a priori.*

The proponents of each language will no doubt insist that I have not even begun to deal with the clinical and theoretical complexities their language has encompassed. Hence, in each case I have failed to reveal the full power of the language. How well I know this! But I would never propose substituting mine for theirs, and I certainly do not propose an eclectic solution. Indeed, finally, I propose no solutions. It is a question of becoming familiar with the various roads and the regions into which they lead us. I deny that the North road is absolutely and for all purposes better than the South; but this is by no means to assert that each is always as good as the other. We need to devise maps showing how each road leads in a genuinely different and interesting direction, though perhaps all happen to intersect at certain places, one of these places being in the region of dynamic insight in psychotherapy.

NOTES

1. Pieter C. Kiors, "The Existential Moment in Psychotherapy," *Journal of Psychology,* XXIV (1961), 153–162.
2. Erich Fromm, *Man for Himself* (New York: Rinehart & Co., 1947), p. 237.

4 / Real Guilt and Neurotic Guilt

Martin Buber, in his discussion of guilt,[1] expressed a justifiable concern that the psychotherapist and the patient may be seduced into diverting attention from the patient's authentic guilt. In order to elaborate upon this concern of his, Buber makes use of a crucial distinction. On the one hand, he speaks of "authentic," "real," "ontic," and, in its most "intense" form, "existential" guilt. On the other hand, there are "neurotic," "psychological," guilt "feelings": the "anxiety-induced bugbears that are generated in the cavern of the unconscious." Neurotic guilt and real guilt, says Buber, are "fundamentally different." [2]

In one form or another, this radical distinction between "real" guilt and "neurotic" guilt feelings has come to play an important role in the discussions among all those European and American psychotherapists who have been influenced either by existentialist or phenomenological or religious outlooks. It is only accurate to add that many psychotherapists in the United States, before they ever became concerned with these philosophical or religious approaches, had individually come to an appreciation of the "reality" of moral and spiritual issues, the one-sidedness of the purely "psychologizing" approach.

But Buber's radical, ontological distinction, though inspired by an important issue, is not the one that the issue demands. Buber's distinction ultimately defeats its own purpose and obscures the psychological facts as well. As a further consequence, it confuses our understanding of the role of the psychotherapist.

The psychotherapist, according to Buber's formulation, is faced with the dilemma of either evading his duty as a human being or overstepping the bounds of psychotherapy proper. Buber tells us that the "significant actuality" transcends the task and methods of the psychotherapist. "Within his methods," says Buber, "the psychotherapist has to do only with guilt feelings, conscious and unconscious. . . ." "But with a comprehensive service to knowledge and help, he must himself encounter guilt as something of an ontic character. . . ." [3]

This dilemma, with the tension it evokes in practice and the problems in theory, is not associated with the problem of guilt alone. The tension pervades therapy because the ontological distinction in question, once enunciated, suggests analogous distinctions throughout the whole range of therapeutic phenomena. Buber's approach makes fundamental and radical a split between the psychotherapeutic treatment proper, now seen as a technical, "scientific" procedure, and the human encounter. Though the distinction may not be offered in this spirit, this is what it requires if taken seriously. Nor is it helpful to "re-mix" the two in practice by telling the therapist that he, at times, "must" go "beyond professional custom and correct methods." [4] This is a practical but anxiety-evoking compromise which leaves things in theoretical confusion; more unfortunate yet, this unhappy compromise is designed to resolve a problem which has been unnecessarily introduced in the first place.

Let me say at once that I do not argue about the validity of distinguishing between guilt associated with neurotic phenomena and guilt which is not thus associated. It is the merit of Buber and others to have used the psychological-ontological distinction as a device to emphasize that there *is* such a thing as real guilt. Buber properly wishes to stress that guilt is a fundamental and inescapable reality of the *normal* person's existence, that it must not be treated by the therapist as something that ought ideally to be "dissolved" entirely before discharging the patient. Yet here is the rub: Buber's invocation of a metaphysical distinction is from the outset a fatal misstep. It is based on a too ready acceptance of the very psychologism to which it is in spirit opposed. Instead of arguing for the unity of human suffering, whether neurotic or otherwise, Buber, in the manner of Descartes, has divided the human world in two. To the technician he assigns a "merely psychological" realm; his own attention then turns to a spiritual realm.

The proper perspective would focus our attention upon the task of achieving personal integrity, not upon dividing man among two realms. With exceptions which do not concern us here, *all* guilt with which we deal should properly be taken as real guilt, as real as any other guilt, and real in the very same sense of "real." Guilt may be assigned by the patient to the wrong source, but that is a common neurotic error which only makes the guilt *seem* foolish. Our responsibility, whether we be concerned with neurotic or non-neurotic aspects of life, is to face our guilt, to accept it, all of it, and, of course, to do something about it if we will. In psychotherapy, what is at stake is not the dissolving of some kind of pseudo-guilt but two other, quite different things: (1) acceptance of the guilt in conjunction with the identification and acknowledgment of its true source in oneself, and (2) a fresh and honest commitment to living openly with that guilt and the self which engenders it, or a new commitment and a reorganization of the self such that we are no longer guilty.

The distinctive characteristic of the neurotic's guilt is not its unreality but, briefly put, its unacknowledged source in infantile, irrational, immoral commitments which are deeply but surreptitiously at the roots of our being. What is "inauthentic" in "neurotic guilt" is not the guilt but the person, for the neurotic pretends to himself and others that there is no good reason for his being guilty. Often he consciously misassigns his felt guilt to some obviously trivial or inappropriate aspect of his life. Then he and others can focus attention on the inappropriateness and the "irrationality" of his feeling guilty—which in turn suggests the desirability of his "dissolving" that feeling. Meanwhile, as the unacknowledged real basis of the guilt, he harbors within himself, however well disguised, desires and aims in violent conflict with the moral order in which, at bottom, he has his being.

The theses I have now presented dogmatically must be elaborated, and certain obvious objections considered.

Guilt is a moral attribute of persons or selves. If we propose to deal with the "fine structure" of guilt, we must be prepared to have to deal with the "fine structure," the "internal structure" of the person. But our ordinary use of the language of guilt is not readily suited to taking into account the internal complexity of the self. We are fluent in talking of guilt only when we are dealing with a reasonably integrated, mature person, or at least with the person viewed as an unanalyzed unit in the particular situation. In such cases we ascribe guilt or not, as the case may be.

But psychotherapists are professionally concerned with viewing a person's actions on a different level. They see action as the outcome of compromises among conflicting tendencies, to some of which the person blinds himself. These conflicting tendencies are quasi-autonomous dynamic complexes of purpose, affect, behavior, thought—indeed of most of the characteristic features of person-hood. They may be thought of, at least for the moment, as *sub-selves*. The word "complex" is too impersonal. Sullivan's term "self-dynamism" is more suggestive, as is Freud's "fantasy-systems"; but "dynamism" and "system" still emphasize the physical metaphor. Now, my object here is not to introduce a new technical conception. It is merely, by the use of the notion "sub-selves," to bring out more forcefully, and informally, the *person*-like features of these sub-unities. The reader can easily translate "sub-self," if he wishes, into the technical language he prefers.

When Freud wrote that ". . . the id knows no values, no good and evil, no morality," [5] he pointed to a crucial characteristic of what I have called the sub-selves (though these are not, of course, identical with what Freud means by the id). To be good and evil, there must be choice. But the sub-selves simply press for expression, each in its own way. They are single-minded, stubborn. And since their single-mindedness is of their essence, they do not of themselves have moral attributes —and this reminds us sharply of a respect in which the sub-selves are only person-*like,* not persons. Somehow, the demands of these various sub-selves and of the perceived environmental demands are weighed; a total response is arrived at. In Freudian theory this latter function is assigned to the judging and executive ego. We need not debate such formulations here. The point is that, however one conceptualizes the matter, the various tendencies to action *are* somehow weighed and combined by a person in his overt action. This capacity lies at the core of what the word "person" designates.

The person faces options, then, and not his sub-selves; therefore the person, not a sub-self, can be guilty.

A person is guilty, says Buber, when he "injures an order of the human world. . . ." We may ask: "Under what conditions does this take place? If the sub-selves do not have moral attributes, what shall we say of the neurotic who is "at the mercy" of some of these sub-selves? If the neurotic is the victim of an uncontrollable sub-self, can the neurotic symptom be a moral crime against the "order of the human world"?

This suggests the first of two common objections to the thesis that neurotic guilt is real guilt. I shall take up both these objections in turn and argue as follows: (1)

It simply will not do to object that the neurotic guilt is unreal because the person was under "inner compulsion" to act wrongly. (2) Nor will it do to say that he is not really guilty since he only wished, or only fantasied, or only symbolically committed the wrong; it will not do, in short, to say he did not literally do what he unconsciously wished to do, so he is not really guilty. Let us consider the first of these objections.

For the purposes of law or other disciplinary action, we may well allow that a neurotic act was "uncontrollable." In legal matters, for example, we may be legitimately interested in hearing testimony that the person acted under the influence of an "uncontrollable impulse."[6] But in psychotherapy, the lesson the patient must learn is that he cannot divest himself of responsibility by allocating such matters to the class of "bugbears generated in the cavern of the unconscious."

Strictly speaking, the psychoneurotic is in therapy not because his basic values are wrong but because a part of him, a sub-self, is surreptitiously dedicated to aims and modes of conduct which betray his basic values. The neurotic's fundamental moral crisis is one of achieving integrity, not one of changing his basic values—though some change in the latter may well be an indirect consequence of having achieved integrity.

The patient in therapy, therefore, must come to see, to experience, to acknowledge with the full vividness of complete and immediate reality his identity with these hitherto unacknowledged, unconscious sub-selves. He must consciously *realize* the extent to which it is, for example, indeed he who, at least with a part of himself, wants to evade responsibility and to be a child, to be loved as a child, or, for example, that it is he who harbors within him murderous impulses toward his father.

Buber's way of viewing the matter leads naturally to his making the seriously misleading statement that "for the patient it is great relief to be diverted from his authentic guilt feeling to an unambiguous neurotic one." [7] But it should not be a "relief" for the patient to discover his "neurotic" guilt; and in fact it is not. The genuine and insightful acknowledgment of guilt by the neurotic is an insight into a burden he has been carrying, is still carrying, a burden from which he may only now, for the first time, be openly and fully suffering. To achieve relief by saying to oneself that it is "only" an irrational neurotic guilt is a therapeutic evasion as well as a spiritual evasion; it is a defense against true insight.

There is a relief which the patient may legitimately enjoy subsequently; but it has a different source. Suppose the patient accepts the guilt and follows this by achieving insight into the motives which engender the guilt; then, at last, the patient may be able decisively to influence those *motives*. Having rejected or transformed those *motives*, he may feel relieved of his burden of guilt.

Of course we know that good therapeutic technique

requires that insight be evoked when that part of the patient which is adult will not be overwhelmed by the experience of guilt. The patient must also be quite aware of other relevant realities, especially that he has in overt deed neither murdered his father nor acted literally as a child. The reasonable adult in the psychoneurotic patient is, after all, the essential therapeutic ally. But it is the first object of insight therapy to enable the patient to accept himself as, in part, unreasonable and childish. I shall come back to these points shortly.

It must be stressed that the person's guilt does not stem merely from the fact that there is a "part" of him, a sub-self, which is irresponsibly infantile. Important as this is, there is another and at least equally important facet to be considered. As we have already noted, sub-selves are not, in themselves, good or evil. It is inevitably the case with the psychoneurotic that, being committed basically to a certain (adult) moral order, he has turned his inward gaze away from the sub-self which is incompatible with that order; but he has done more than avert his gaze: he has then *surreptitiously cooperated.* After all, the sub-self is not a "part" of the person in some mechanical or physical sense of "part." To be a "part" of a *person* is in essence to be in some way accepted as such by the person, to be identified with by the person. The spectrum of neurotic symptomatology is simply the spectrum of those surreptitious alliances between the person and his unacknowledged sub-selves. Where we do not suppose such a surreptitious alliance, we do not speak of neurotic symptoms. Instead, if there is malfunctioning, we speak in non-purposive terms of organic malfunction. Thus the neurotic person is guilty, really guilty, because of this surreptitious alliance with that in himself which aims at injuring "an order of the human world whose foundations he knows and recognizes as those of his own existence. . . ."[8]

The analogy of parent and child may help here—indeed it is more than a mere analogy. Though a parent acknowledges his child's cruel actions and takes steps to prevent them, he may still be held *legally* responsible for the acts of his minor ward. In this case, however, his neighbors do not usually hold the parent to be morally guilty—though we shall have more to say about this shortly. On the other hand, if the parent averts his eyes, and if he surreptitiously arranges opportunities for sadistic acts by the child, then the parent is morally guilty.

Pressing the analogy one step further, we ask: How, if he will, can the parent effectively and humanely deal with the cruelty of his child? If the parent is not to treat the child merely as a target of condemnation or as an inconvenient object, he must to some extent be able to identify himself with the child. If he can tolerate doing this, his stronger and more mature ego may, in alliance with the child's healthy impulses, help find the way to a legitimate resolution of the problem. The parent-child relationship is a symbiotic one in which the weaker, allied with the stronger, moves gradually toward differentiation and genuine independence. The theoretical implications of the parent-child symbiosis hypothesis are consistent with the commonly observed clinical facts. It is a clinical commonplace to find that the parent of an abnormally sadistic child—to continue with this example—has subtly encouraged the child's sadism. The parent evades overt expression of his own sadism through identification with the child. It is this symbiotic aspect of parent-child relations and its roots in identification which completes the parallelism between parent-child and person-sub-self. For, just as we are morally guilty for the sub-selves which we consciously deny, so the parent, through identification, is guilty for the sadistic acts which he has conspired to encourage but which he consciously condemns. In both types of cases, the source of the guilt may not be consciously or correctly known by the person himself, but that source is often easily detectable by the therapist.

The phrase "neurotic guilt" is, then, a handy but misleading metonomy referring to the (genuine) guilt of a neurotic person. It is not unreal because done "under compulsion." The similarity between compulsiveness and compulsion, so illuminating in many contexts, should not blind us to their crucial difference. When I act "under compulsion," it is *really another person* who dominates me. But when I act "compulsively," it is a part of myself, a sub-self with whose demands I surreptitiously identify myself, that dominates. "Neurotic guilt" is the guilt of a person self-blinded, afraid, and secretly untrue to his own adult commitment. "Authentic guilt" is no more authentic as *guilt;* it is the person who acts more authentically toward the guilt by fully acknowledging it and its source.

We turn now to the second objection mentioned earlier: Since the neurotic has merely "fantasied" or only symbolically gratified the demands of the infantile subselves, is not his guilt, too, merely a "fantasy," an "illusory" guilt? After all, even if he has indulged, for example, in surreptitious minor aggressions against a father figure, these are far from literal patricide. Disguised and socially accepted forms of dependence on another person are not *literally* the same as acting like a child. Disguised incestuous fantasies are a far cry from literally incestuous acts. The potencies claimed in the neurotic's conscious and unconscious fantasies are precisely the impotencies of his "real" life. Why, if this is all "wishful thinking," is the neurotic *really* guilty?

Here I shall have to state a general thesis first, and then introduce two important qualifications. When stated bluntly, the general thesis still often appears novel and radical. Yet this very thesis is fundamental to twentieth-century dynamic psychiatry and, equally, to the historic moral insights of the major civilizations.[9] The thesis, briefly, is this: moral guilt accrues by virtue of our wishes, not merely our acts. Of course, legal guilt depends primarily upon our acts, though we should note that even here the assessment of motive plays a role. But the question of moral guilt does not wait for acts; it is in profound degree a question of what one harbors in one's heart. This is the gist of Freud's basic concept of "psychic reality." In the psychic economy, the wish is omnipotent. To wish is, psychologically, to have done. Hence a person suffers guilt for his wishes, even his unconscious ones.

This insight, so central to dynamic psychiatry, is not in opposition to the central insights of the great moral teachings. It is ironic that, important as psychotherapists know "matters of the mind" to be, they are still tempted to assume naïvely, as if it were all self-evident, that, morally speaking, "mere" wishes do not count. A wish, morally speaking, seems to them to be "*only* a matter of the mind." This may be because the explicit use of moral language in "scientifically" oriented circles has come to be abandoned to the social critic, the disciplinarian, or the judge—in general, those responsible primarily for controlling or guiding action. The explicit analysis of *personal* morality has tended to be unfashionable and associated with religion, Victorian prissiness, or puritanical rigidity. The sources of this error are no doubt complex, and the psychiatrist's contact with neurotic pseudo-moralizing has not been the most encouraging context in which to take the study of moral language seriously. Whatever the reasons, the fact is that most psychotherapists, in their informal and formal discussions, tacitly assume that only actions and their effects, viewed "literally" and not "symbolically," are what count morally. Since this assumption is made, even though tacitly, we must at least briefly note that, far from being self-evident, it runs counter to central teachings in the great moral traditions.

Jesus taught—and it is central to his teaching—"Ye have heard it was said by them of old time, Thou shalt not commit adultery. . . . But I say unto you that whosoever looketh on a woman to lust after her hath committed adultery with her already in his heart." [10] Jesus did not deny the importance of the law and of works; but the life with which he was primarily concerned was that of the spirit. This religious-moral insight is congruent with Freud's discovery that it was fantasy, not only actions, which had shaped the character and the fate of his patients.

If we turn to the East, we find that the Bhagavad Gita has taught the Indian peoples that it is to the desires, the motives, and not to the actions, that we must look when we wish to diagnose the spiritual condition of an individual. As for Buddhism, the great Buddhist moral tract, the Dhammapada, begins quite characteristically: "All that we are is the result of what we have thought: it is founded on our thoughts, it is made up of our thoughts." And in the same chapter: "Those who are thoughtless are as if dead already."[11] Confucius, the great advocate of ritual and tradition, differed from his predecessors precisely in his teaching that it is the inner spirit which is crucial in the carrying out of ritual, that, indeed, in the last analysis, the inward virtues would of themselves be morally definitive if the external world were to prevent one from displaying these virtues in action.[12]

It is, then, not at all self-evident that the wish which is not literally gratified leaves one morally "clean," though perhaps psychically disturbed. On the contrary, the burden of proof lies the other way. Psychotherapists often claim an aversion to introducing moral and philosophical assumptions into their professional doctrine, but the fact is that they do, and the present dubious assumption is a case in point.

Two qualifying comments are necessary with regard to the thesis that, in the moral life, the wish establishes guilt or innocence. The first comment is really not so much a qualification as an explicit statement of what is *not* implied by that thesis. The thesis that one only need wish evil in order to be genuinely guilty is perfectly consistent with the fact that it is worse to commit a real murder than it is to fantasy committing one. To deny this would indeed be to fly in the face of sanity. The question is: In what ways is the one worse than the other?

Part of the answer is obvious and important; but since it is one without any further theoretical interest to us,

I shall merely mention it and then go on to the rest of the answer. It is worse to act on an evil wish than it is merely to fantasy the gratification of the wish because the actual suffering inflicted on others is itself an additional evil to cherishing the wish alone. We cannot measure the difference, but the point needs no laboring. This fact is reason enough to entitle us to make vastly different *practical* judgments regarding the actual murderer on the one hand, and, on the other, the neurotic with murderous fantasies (even if these are incorporated in symbolic form in action).

In addition to the social evil of its consequences, however, the overt act increases the evil in another way, a way which is of distinct theoretical interest to us here. The overt commission of the deed by the murderer is the mark of the person's decisive acceptance of the wish. The moral significance of the degree of acceptance becomes clearer when we consider the case of a murderer who was inwardly in great conflict before the decision. Our conviction that there was such conflict tempers our judgment of his guilt, though it in no sense absolves him of it. The neurotic with unconscious murderous wishes is a person who differs from the murderer in this respect: though beset by the demands of a sub-self, he is a person who successfully fights against accepting the demand in its flagrant form. And he does this precisely because overt gratification would rupture the order of the world to which he is basically committed.

Up to this point in my argument, I have emphasized the complicity of the person in his neurosis. But the reverse of the coin is his successful refusal to give in entirely, his refusal to make an open alliance, his temporizing, emasculating, suppressing tactics toward the immoral sub-self. The person who is psychoneurotic in the classical sense of that term is fitted for insight therapy precisely because he is, for the most part, a person committed in deed as well as intent to fighting, however irrationally, the infantile and irresponsible demands of his sub-selves. This fight *is* the neurotic conflict.

We can now see that when the murder is actually committed, the person's burden of guilt is greater than the neurotic's because the acceptance of the murderous wish is more wholehearted; the person has more fully identified himself with the murderous sub-self. And yet, unless he is a psychopath, he may still have to recognize that he has "injured an order of the human world whose foundations he knows and recognizes as those of his own existence." The neurotic, on the other hand, is tempted to murder, but, *on the whole,* he elects decisively not to give in. (And then, as the neurotic symptom shows, he compromises and distorts, and cooperates *to a limited extent,* via the back door, as it were, with the evil he has cast out from the front.) Genuine reluctance to be an accomplice in evil ameliorates guilt just as, for example, *genuine* repentance does—these are facts of the moral life, and also of the psychology of grief and repentance.

Let us return to our essential theme: though we deal with varying degrees of guilt, it is all guilt in the same sense; in the moral, or, if you wish, the existential sense. What is more, the guilt with which we are here concerned is, in practice, guilt in substantial degree. Though the guilt for murderous fantasies may be less in degree than for actual murder, the phrase "less in degree" in these matters does not imply inconsequential. For the neurotic it is not inconsequential. How do we weigh the degree of guilt? The matter, for our purposes, is simple. The neurotic, though maintaining his repressive distortions successfully, may still be so guilty that his life is ruined and his moral fate a tragic one. The special pathos of the neurotic's fate is that the source of the guilt is not understood, its legitimacy often doubly obscured by displacement to venial sins, misdemeanors, nonsense-acts. Not only the amount of suffering and its apparent meaninglessness, but also the degree of irrationality of the defensive maneuvers is a measure of the degree of that guilt. In general, it is clear that the neurotic does not have to act in order to bring his *real* guilt to a burdensome, even a crippling level. He may "do" nothing; yet it may be that, like the Pharisees, his "inward part is full of ravening and wickedness." [13] It is a remarkable error indeed that psychotherapists could deny the genuinely *moral* character of the corruption which is an inward fact just because it has no direct outward expression.

There is, then, no puzzling metaphysical gap between

"neurotic guilt" and ontic guilt. The therapist *is* always dealing with what Buber calls the "significant actuality." It is worth repeating that the great value of Buber's ontological distinction is to force us to acknowledge that there *is* a "significant actuality" involved in life and in therapy. But, this lesson once learned, it is time to go further. It is time to see that most of the guilt which is ordinarily considered within the scope of the therapist's "professional custom and correct methods" *is* the significant actuality, not a subjective, half-real, sub-human phenomenon.

We must now take a moment to ask: Is there no possibility of "feeling" guilty when one is not actually guilty? Are there not some forms of pathology in which the "feeling" may arise independently of a sub-self whose demands violate the moral order? This question raises a host of problems, both psychological and philosophical. Fortunately we need not deal with them here because, in order to simplify the analysis, I have restricted the applicability of my theses to adult psychoneurotics. The guilt feelings of the psychoneurotic are ordinarily associated with unconscious sub-selves which strive against the "order of the human world whose foundations he knows and recognizes as those of his own existence." The generic motive of repression—as against conscious suppression of impulses—is that the inner demands are apprehended to be such that to face them openly would be to threaten one's integrity. The demands the neurotic represses are infantile in character. Hence they are incompatible with adult responsibility as well as too primitive in quality to be acceptable. The sub-self which the person can see how to integrate into his world is one which he will face and accept consciously. But where no solution even seems possible, then repression is instituted. Even where there is no conscious guilt feeling, it must be assumed that there is some guilt associated with repression in the neurotic. It is here that Freud and others have been forced to speak apologetically of "unconscious guilt." This is because they really mean to refer guilt to the *fact* of radical inner conflict, but they also still think that guilt is simply a *feeling* and hence must, by definition, be *felt*. But feeling or no feeling, the therapist expects that "moral anxiety" will be a significant element in psychopathology except in cases where he assumes the patient to be radically immature or defective in a way which excludes him from the classification "adult psychoneurotic."

The absence in the literature of clear-cut examples illustrating the supposed radical distinction between neurotic and existential guilt is good evidence, I hold, that there is no such ontological distinction to be observed. I myself have read the words but have looked often and vainly for illustrations which decisively differentiate the two kinds of guilt. I see in the literature exhortations to make the distinction unaccompanied by usable criteria for making it. Only the theoretical prejudice that the psychological is the "merely" psychological has forced people into this radical verbal dualism in order to preserve the insight, a re-discovery in a new context, that there is really a moral dimension to life. What we must now see, in addition, is that *all* insight therapy has the moral dimension. The only illusion involved in connection with neurotic guilt is the self-deception of the neurotic as to the occasion of his guilt.

I believe that the analysis I have presented preserves continuity in psychotherapeutic theory in place of introducing metaphysical chasms. It is consistent with the moral insights of the great moral teachers as well as the psychological insights of dynamic psychiatry. It emphasizes the human dignity of the totality of the neurotic's suffering, the reality of his spiritual problem. In addition to each of these, the view I have presented clarifies the relation of the psychotherapist to the spiritual adviser or to the wise and good friend. The psychotherapist is never merely a technician but is *always* a person in an encounter with another human being who is bearing genuinely human burdens. The therapist, however, is specially experienced and skilled in connection with one form of human burden. The therapist is concerned, generally, with the failures of the person to achieve or maintain the integrity of the inner community of sub-selves. More specifically, however, he is concerned with these failures insofar as they rely on self-deception, either with regard to the realities of the "external" world or the realities of the "inner" world. The psychotherapist is an expert—insofar as one can be "expert" in human affairs—on the conditions, the motives, and the devices associated with self-deceptive evasion of the world in which one has one's being.

This view of therapy is, I believe, in the same spirit, though not quite the same theoretical framework, as that of Buber's views on the matter.

NOTES

1. Martin Buber, "Guilt and Guilt Feelings," *Psychiatry,* XX (1957), 114–129.
2. *Ibid.,* p. 117.
3. *Ibid.,* p. 115.
4. *Ibid.,* p. 117.
5. Sigmund Freud, *New Introductory Lectures on Psychoanalysis* (New York: W. W. Norton & Co., 1933), p. 105.
6. See E. Madden, "Psychoanalysis and Moral Judgeability," *Philosophy and Phenomenological Research,* XVIII (1957), 68–79.
7. Buber, *op. cit.,* p. 117.
8. *Loc. cit.*
9. See Herbert Fingarette, "Psychoanalytic Perspectives on Moral Guilt and Responsibility: A Reevaluation," *Philosophy and Phenomenological Research,* XVI (1955), 18–36.
10. Matthew 5:27–28.
11. "Dhammapada," in Lin Yutang, *The Wisdom of China and India* (New York: Modern Library, 1942), pp. 327–328.
12. See, for one of many examples, Confucius, *Analects,* 7:15.
13. Luke 11:39.

5 / From Oedipus to Orestes: A Paradigm of Becoming Responsible

In the art and drama of ancient Greece, the story of Orestes ranked at least equal in significance to that of Oedipus. In our own times, however, it is the story of Orestes which has served as a main plot for such writers as O'Neill,[1] Eliot,[2] and Sartre.[3] On the other hand the emphasis in the psychoanalytic literature has been the other way around: It is Oedipus' story, as we know, which has occupied the center of the stage. The result, though little noted, is worth attention: though *extant* texts have often been interpreted in terms of the Oedipus paradigm, the *new* works have been written with explicit use of the Orestes paradigm.

This is a symptom not in itself so important, but it is of the greatest importance for what it signals. One wonders whether, in failing to read the Orestes story aright or to appreciate its significance, psychoanalysts may have failed to read some main intellectual movements of our times aright. And likewise, if there is a possible psychoanalytic reading of Orestes which shows it to be of central importance, this may exhibit in a fresh way the bearing of psychoanalysis on our mid-century movements of thought. It is my thesis that the correct reading is just such a reading.

There are a few psychoanalytic or quasi-psychoanalytic discussions of Orestes.[4–9] For the most part they present his story as a "homosexual" variant on the Oedipus story. Such an interpretation, however, is quite out of gear with the main drift of the Orestes story. Nor is it helpful to diagnose Orestes as a case of "dementia praecox," as did an early student of the subject. Though interesting points have been made in these discussions, the profound and main psychological significance of the story has been missed or placed in the wrong context. More important: this failure has not been the result of accident or unperceptiveness, though the Orestes motif has a psychological significance exactly equal to that of the Oedipus motif; indeed it is the complement of the latter. The motif of the Oedipus story crystallized Freud's first great insights into the early development of the instinctual drives; the motif of the Orestes story crystallizes out the much later insights concerning the ego and superego. Only with a clear fundamental grasp of the large, constructive import of these later conceptions—what has since blossomed into psychoanalytic "ego-psychology"—could a truly modern psychoanalytic analysis of Orestes be carried out. The carrying out of such an analysis is the main task of the present discussion.

I have mentioned the fact that the Orestes motif links psychoanalysis and other main movements of modern thought. An additional virtue of a correct analysis of Orestes' story lies in its unifying power within psychoanalytic theory. For the story then forms a framework within which to see how the new ego-psychology is organically related to the earlier insights, especially those concerning the Oedipal conflict.

I would like to make it clear that I do not suppose that I am going to give *the* "real" meaning of the Orestes story in presenting a psychoanalytical account. Nor am I engaged in a treasure hunt for choice "symbols" or other miscellaneous items "of psychoanalytic interest." The elements in isolation are of little psychoanalytic interest; we must see how they function within a large pattern. In saying that great mythic drama such as Aeschylus' *Oresteia* has profundity, richness, and perennial powers of illumination, we are necessarily saying that it does *not* have only one meaning. Such works have many dimensions of meaning; these interlock in such a way as to form a dense, meaning-packed unity. Explications of *a* meaning, such as the one I shall give, are to be tested by reference to this unity.

The specific unity which guides me in the following is that of Aeschylus' trilogy, the *Oresteia,* taken with due regard for its setting, and with special reference to Orestes himself.[10–25] I shall present the evidence for a psychoanalytic interpretation which fits squarely into the main drift of the Orestes story in its many dimensions, an interpretation which locks in with the story as we intuitively and directly know it. What I elaborate here —for the most part quite single-mindedly—is simply psychological content or meaning. Toward the latter part of my discussion, I shall refer briefly to literary, religious, historical, and other dimensions of its meaning. Some final brief reference to twentieth-century versions of the Orestes story will be the basis for completing the discussion.

I

We must begin with some very brief remarks on the story of Oedipus the King. It is, psychologically, the essential background against which the Orestes story begins. As we recall, Oedipus has a fate announced by the oracles: he is to kill his father and marry his mother. This he eventually does, not until later realizing what he has done. Upon seeing the true nature of his deeds, he tears out his eyes and takes himself into exile.

This story reflects the psychic pattern which was one of Freud's earliest and greatest discoveries. The male infant is destined to achieve his first genuine psychic unity, his person-hood, in a psychic world which consists of self and family, and at a phase when he is dominated by erotic impulses toward the mother and destructive impulses toward the "rival" father. This is all a matter of unconscious fantasy; we see normally only the distorted derivatives of it in conscious fantasy and in conduct. In actuality, the psychic relationships are far more complex than this first simple formula suggests; the fear and rejections which are inevitable produce still further complications. The whole constitutes the Oedipal conflict—a pattern with as many individual variants as there are individual human beings.

This Oedipal conflict is the "fate" of the male child; yet, as in the Sophocles play, it is a fate which is not something "externally" imposed, nor is it magic or miracle. In the play and in life, it is simply the fate, foreknown to those who already "see," which the individual himself brings about by his own actions, actions which then have their natural consequences. To be told of this "fate" is ineffectual in preventing it; it is mere words. Each one must go through the experience in order to learn its lesson. The play portrays clearly and in a moment what the real-life child only apprehends dimly and deals with over time.

In any case, the essence of the matter for our purposes is this: this is an insight into an impossible situation, a situation which is disastrous if not remedied. Insight, we know now, does not magically solve problems. To see what one has done or is doing is merely the basis for a solution; it is not itself the solution. We cannot evade the task of inventing and adopting a constructive *response* to the situation into which we have the insight.

The Oedipus story, then, presents the central conflict of personal development *from a certain perspective:* the perspective is that of the pre-Oedipal child who is moving *into* the central Oedipal conflict. The Oedipus story ends with the insight into the meaning of this line of movement. This movement has led to a situation which is radically unsatisfactory, one which also appears to be a dead end.

What happens next? What happens as seen from the perspective of one who successfully moves *through* the conflict and *on out of it*? Here is where the psychological content of the Orestes story merges with that of Oedipus' story. For Orestes is just such a one. Oedipus and Orestes represent, psychologically, one individual: Oedipus is the individual as he moves *into* the central growth crisis; Orestes is the individual as he moves out of it. Oedipus exhibits man's psychic bondage, the "acts" in which are the roots of his damnation; Orestes exhibits man's liberation, the task whose fruits are salvation and harmony. There is no doubt that the over-all theme of the *Oresteia* is one of salvation, harmony, liberation. Let us now see in some detail, then, how Orestes does play the psychological and dramatic role I have suggested.

We leave Oedipus as one who exiles himself in horror from the scene of his crime, one who shudders with repugnance before his murder-based claim to his father's throne and to his mother as wife. Orestes, the young man, is introduced upon the stage as one who returns from exile to his royal home, one who shudders in horror at the murder of his father and the quasi-incestuous liaison of his mother with Aegisthus, her co-conspirator in the killing. Orestes was a young boy at the time. Now, a manly youth, he returns.

Orestes, then, is coming back to the Oedipal situation. Only now he comes as destroyer, purifier, liberator.

Oedipus committed his criminal acts out of natural impulse and temptation. He was fated to do as he did. Orestes is a man who does not have a fate, but a *destiny*. The difference is vital. Orestes is in plain fact the son and heir of the house of Atreus; but it is still necessary that he *take up* the responsibilities of this role. He could, if he chose, remain an exile, a man who was no one and belonged nowhere. Apollo's oracle told him that if he did not take up his responsibility, he would suffer from decay of spirit, sickness of body, and the rejection of men. Death—on every level of existence—is the wages of evasion of his responsibility. But in the *Oresteia* it is quite clear that this is a responsibility which Orestes can refuse to accept. It is neither a necessity, nor, obviously, is it an arbitrary whim of the god's, a command having no real basis in Orestes' life. Orestes has, however, made a *vow* to Apollo, the purifier, to accept his responsibility as son and heir. It is his own vow which binds him. And of course it is in coming to bind ourselves in *this* way that we begin to exercise our freedom.

It is of interest to notice what psychological dynamics are expressed in the setting of the Orestes story. The *repression* of the Oedipal impulses is represented by the fact that Orestes enters upon a family scene whose crimes are not only not his but also occurred long ago. The Oedipal role of the son, since it cannot be taken by Orestes, is projected onto a suitable substitute: the weak and womanish Aegisthus, former exile, rival and murderer of his uncle, Agamemnon, and lover of his aunt, Clytemnestra. The conscious feelings of Orestes as he deliberates upon the situation are precisely what we should expect. He feels repugnance toward Aegisthus, the Oedipal self to be destroyed. He feels reverence and love tinged with awe of the father, once his rival, now to be his spiritual ally. And he is torn with inner conflict by the solemn necessity, which he acknowledges, to destroy the faithless mother. For though she is his mother, she is an erotic temptress, and she is also a dominating and powerful woman, a dangerous obstacle to Orestes' assuming power in his own right.

> . . . *Yet I must do this deed* [says Orestes]. *To this one end my will is urged by many motives: the God's command, grief for my father; and with these the loss of my patrimony; shame that my proud citizens . . . are thus enslaved to a woman—no, to a pair of women! Aegisthus! Woman or man, he shall learn his lesson now.*[26]

From the standpoint of the psychological content of the story, the first action which Orestes must take is evident. We know that the young boy in real life must propitiate the father whom he in Oedipal fantasy destroys; he must now turn to the father in a new way, establish him as a source of strength, as an ally. This is not merely an alliance between two flesh-and-blood males; even more fundamentally, it is an intimate alliance in which the *spirit* of the father is established in a place of honor and authority within the boy's psyche. The father now speaks through the son, and the latter, in turn, becomes the legitimate heir. In psychoanalytic language: the son identifies with the father, his former rival, and the introjected image of the father becomes the core of the boy's superego.

Orestes' first entrance on stage is as a suppliant come to accomplish just this end: in solemn ritual he places two locks of his hair on his father's grave. One expresses his grief and, we may speculate, appeasement; the other represents his new status as a youth just coming of age. After Electra and Orestes have recognized each other, there begins a long series of incantatory chants in which

Orestes, his sister Electra, and the Chorus appeal to the spirit of the murdered Agamemnon. Orestes' appeal expresses the very elements of the psychological pattern we have just considered:

> *Father* [cries Orestes], *your own son calls you: stand at my side! . . . Give me, I pray, this throne and kingdom, yours by right. . . . Save us, and the due ritual feasts shall be established for you. . . . You are dead—and yet not dead: still you can live in us.*[27]

And, in offering the two locks of hair at his father's grave, Orestes had said:

> *I call on my dead father to hear, to sanction. . . . Now I am a man. . . .*[28]

The great length of the suppliant prayers at the father's grave is a feature of Aeschylus' play which has been criticized as dramatically questionable. The psychological perspective helps us to see how it is dramatically justified. It is true that we do not have the dance and the music which must have originally accompanied this long prayer scene. But we cannot suppose Aeschylus let the story merely mark time in order to make room for a song-and-dance interlude. We must suppose that the dramatic forces at work *required* expression in an elaborate performance calling for the combined resources of language, music, and dance. To understand the Aeschylus *Oresteia* we must appreciate the portentousness of this phase of the dramatic development. And this development must have its basis in the psychological content as well as in the other dimensions of the play's meaning. We must sense the awesomeness and power which Agamemnon, even dead, still has for Orestes; we must recall the way men still tremble at the thought of Agamemnon's wrath, marvel at his glory and fame, quake at the forces which his aroused spirit might set into motion. Then we grasp the rhythm and force of this long, great prayer by King Agamemnon's tomb.

> Clearly [says Freud] the repression of the Oedipus complex was no easy task. . . . [The child's ego] borrowed strength to do this, so to speak, from the father, and this loan was an extraordinarily momentous event.[29]

Orestes' second main task is twofold: he must destroy his powerful mother, and he must destroy her weak and treacherous lover, Aegisthus. His reasons are several: (a) the woman who was a treacherous wife and illicit lover must be destroyed; (b) he must, as the heir, take over the lawful rule of the community, free the community from the "female" domination of the usurpers (Aegisthus is several times called a woman for his weak use of guile rather than open confrontation); (c) Aegisthus must be destroyed as the contemptible creature he is.

These motives correspond to those which move the

young male in the course of resolving Oedipal conflict and reaching a fundamentally new psychic organization. He must not only identify with the father, but also, as main tasks: (a) he must eliminate the image of the mother as object of erotic and illicit love, thus freeing himself for non-incestuous and non-competitive love attachments, (b) he must break free from his infantile dependence on the mother, thus decisively establishing his own autonomy and his own maleness; (c) by doing these things, he eliminates the fantasies of himself in the role of mother's consort and father's usurper.

Is there no moral conflict over these killings by Orestes? And, psychologically, is there no psychic conflict in the young male? The answer is not simple. The killing of Aegisthus presents no conflict to Orestes; there is a "moral pleasure" in destroying so contemptible a creature. "*His* death gets no word from me," [30] says Orestes curtly. This corresponds to the psychological point that the Oedipal self and its fantasies must be decisively abandoned. Just because of this, however, any fixation, or any repression of the Oedipal wish evokes intense repressive forces, the conscious experience being that extreme repugnance which the normal person feels toward incest.

The killing of Clytemnestra, however, poses a more formidable problem. She is, after all, Orestes' own mother. She bore him, nursed him—and, for a while, no doubt she loved and was loved by him. She is a strong woman, man-like in her force of will and mind. When Orestes has at last slain Aegisthus, Clytemnestra rushes upon the scene and reacts toward Orestes with two quite different gestures in turn.

Her first response upon seeing Orestes standing with bloody sword over the slain Aegisthus is to cry out in grief and fury. "Bring me my man-slaying axe!" [31] she cries to the attendants; but it is too late. (We might note that the central psychological threat at this phase of maturation is the threat of castration; and, aside from her evident aggressiveness, the specific weapon Clytemnestra chooses, unlike Orestes' sword, is particularly expressive of this theme.)

Clytemnestra, unable to get a weapon and immediately having gained better possession of her emotions, changes her approach. Now she makes a new dramatic appeal. The appeal which comes at this point and the imagery in which it is cast are ubiquitous in the Greek variants of the Orestes story. She falls to her knees and cries: "My own child, see this breast: here often your head lay, in sleep, while your soft mouth sucked from me the good milk that gave you life and strength." [32]

Thus, Clytemnestra turns to what is psychologically the most archaic and profound of images. "A child's first erotic object is the mother's breast that feeds him." [33] The bond signified in this image is, as Freud said, prototypical; it is the bond upon which later love for the mother and dependence upon her are modeled.[34]

Now, perversely, Clytemnestra uses this prototypical bond for the purpose of perpetuating her domination of Orestes. But she herself has unwittingly contributed to making the moment decisive by her earlier and self-betraying threat. "In males . . . the threat of castration brings the Oedipus complex to an end," says Freud.[35]

Nevertheless, at this juncture, for the first and only time during the play, Orestes genuinely hesitates. "Pylades!," he cries out to the hitherto silent companion of his travels—"Pylades, what shall I do? To kill a mother is terrible. Shall I show mercy?" [36] Everything depends on Orestes' next act.

Pylades, who by name, origin, and function in the play represents Apollo, now utters the only lines he has in the play. They are few, but decisive:

> *Where then are Apollo's words, his Pythian oracles? What become of men's sworn oaths? Make all men living your enemies, but not the gods.*[37]

This is the moment, then, when the most awe-ful and shocking of crimes is to be committed out of a moral and spiritual necessity. Of course Orestes already has weighty reasons for doing what he is about to do; of course he knows that he has previously bound himself to do it in sacred oath. He knows what he must do, and yet—"to kill a mother is terrible."

What is needed in such momentous action is support from the very deepest sources of strength, sources which transcend the realm of the voluntary, the conscious, the planned. Nothing but the very voice of the divine will swing the balance. Here, too, a profound psychological truth is expressed: This, says Freud, is a "struggle which [rages] in the deepest strata of the mind." [38] And as to these deepest sources of the youth's masculinity: "for our knowledge it is something ultimate . . . [it is a] problem which clearly falls entirely within the province of biology." [39]

In both the Orestes myth and the psychoanalytical formulation, the decisive forces at the critical moment transcend the conscious and voluntary; they surge out of the depths (or heights) which activate man but which are not controlled by him.

Yet we do not deal here with a complete subjection to forces beyond us. Orestes is not *forced* to go ahead: "I uphold your judgment," [40] he replies to Pylades, and then, of his own volition, does go ahead. Analogously, the decisive balance of psychological forces is not, for Freud, *merely* a matter of biology. The fact is that he speaks again and again in terms of struggle, will, mastery. The ego must "properly master the Oedipus complex." [41] Or again, more plainly, in speaking of the therapy of the neurotic (who, after all, is belatedly dealing with these same problems), Freud says the neurotic

> must find the *courage* to *direct his attention* to the phenomena of his illness. His illness itself must no longer seem to

> him *contemptible,* but *must become* an *enemy* wor
> his mettle. . . .[42]

And in speaking directly of the way we react to our own residual Oedipus complex in seeing the Sophocles *Oedipus Rex,* Freud assures us that we cannot ascribe it all to the unconscious and absolve ourselves of responsibility:

> "In vain do you deny that you are accountable. . . ."

> [we] are compelled to feel [our] responsibility in the form of a sense of guilt for which [we] can discern no foundation.[43]

How can the deed be one in which the individual accepts responsibility, *is* responsible, and yet is moved by forces which transcend his control? The question is fundamental, and the answer is at best complex when not entirely shrouded in mystery. But the task of clarification is not one we need take up here. The point which we must note is that the paradox holds *equally* in the psychoanalytic account of the matter *and* explicitly in the *Oresteia.* The form of the paradox in the one mirrors the form in the other. Furthermore it is a distinctive paradox. It is central to every doctrine in which personal responsibility dwells side by side with the operation of forces transcending the conscious will. The Orestes story brings out the paradox sharply, and thus it frames for us a central paradox in the psychology of the individual's "coming of age" as well as in the notion of responsibility itself.

Freud summarizes what I would call the Orestean task in the following words:

> . . . the human individual must devote himself to the great task of *freeing himself from the parents;* and only after this detachment is accomplished can he cease to be a child and so become a member of the social community. For a son, the task consists in releasing his libidinal desires from his mother, in order to employ them in the quest of an external love object in reality; and in reconciling himself with his father if he has remained antagonistic to him. . . .[44]

The Orestean resolution of the Oedipal conflict is achieved, then, by the establishment of a powerful and independent ego inwardly guided and supported by the paternal superego, freed of the unsublimated libidinal attachment to the mother and the childhood dependence on her, ready for new cathexes of new objects and tasks in the real "social community" as replacements for those of the child's world of fantasy and family.

Such a radical transformation of one's world and of the roles of the persons in it is not painless; it involves much guilt and inner turmoil. Prior to his deeds, Orestes shows this inner turmoil most explicitly whenever he thinks of his mother *as* his mother rather than as merely a destined target of destruction. When he is told of the dream of Clytemnestra, that she gave birth to a snake which bit her breast while she nursed it, he sees the point at once:

> *It means that she who nursed this obscene beast must die by violence; I must transmute my nature, be viperous in heart and act! The dream commands it: I am her destined murderer.*[45]

We see that Orestes is not ruthless; nor is he acting as he does out of sly calculation or a narrow hope of saving his skin. He groans at what he must do; he is even ready to lose his own life for such a deed:

> *And when her life is ended; Let mine be cast away.*[46]

We know—though Orestes has no such ulterior motive—that dying to the old life precedes being born to the new.

In analyzing the exile, torment, and purification which actually do follow the Orestean deed, we must recall that, psychologically, this is never accomplished in one stroke. The initial phase, in the pre-latency period of childhood, is only the first in a series of eruptions of this conflict. This first stage, at about ages three to five, issues in a turning away in the "exile" of latency to two sorts of new tasks. One is learning to live as this new Orestean self, learning to come to terms with this new resolution of the old conflict. At this age, the coming to terms consists in establishing the core of the new relationships to the family and self while using primarily repressive defenses against the upsurge of the old. The second sort of task in latency is an "outwardly" oriented one: the child learns to join the "social community" as a social being, learns necessary social skills, schools its intellect. The child, in short, wanders through the outer world, as does Orestes after his murders. He is an exile, "long wandering through tribes and towns . . . welcoming homes." [47] He meets new "friends whose homes and hands have given me welcome without harm or taint." [48]

The second great stage of Oedipal conflict and its Orestean resolution is the stormy period of adolescence. At this time, the old instinctual drives take on a new force, old wounds and old temptations sorely try the young male; again he must take on the responsibility and reassume in a new context the burdens of the Orestean task. He must deepen anew the identification with the father, put away decisively the tempting and dominating mother, become his father's heir rather than his rival, and seek an independent life in the world. During this second stormy "exile" from home and into the world, he is more decisively concerned with purging the archaic guilt rather than merely repressing it. The ideal is a full dissolution of the Oedipal conflict, a genuine *purification* rather than a violent overthrow and repression of the residual old loyalties. "Long wandering through tribes and towns has cleansed my bloodstained hand, blunted the edge of guilt." [49] And Freud stressed that until the ego has "properly mastered the Oedipus complex," [50] the residue of the old conflict will also involve that tension between ego and superego which is moral "impurity," i.e., guilt.[51]

Finally, Orestes is able to say to the court in Athens at which he arrives after many years to be judged:

> *The blood upon my hand is drowsed and quenched; the stain of matricide washed clean. . . . And now from holy lips, with pure words, I invoke Athene. . . .*[52]

Still other essential elements in the psychological pattern are to be noted in connection with Orestes' exile after the murder. There is nothing more appropriate to the period after the loss of the mother than an element of mourning. And indeed Freud speaks [53] of the giving up of the early sexual object as linked not only to the sublimation of the instincts and to the formation of character, but also to a phase akin to mourning. Blos, in his recent psychoanalytic study of adolescence, summarizes the psychoanalytic account as follows:

> The infantile sexual tie has to be irrevocably severed. . . .[54]

> The object loss which the adolescent experiences in relation to the parent of his childhood, that is, in relation to the parent image, contains features of mourning. This adolescent

> loss is more final and irrevocable than the one which occurs at the end of the oedipal phase. Root has shown that "the work of mourning is an important psychological task in the period of adolescence." . . . It accounts in part for the depressive states of adolescence, as well as for their grief reaction as a postponement of affect. To complete the work of mourning requires repetition and time.[55]

Perhaps it is appropriate to take note here of the fact that Apollo, Orestes' "sponsor," is explicitly and emphatically identified not only as the representative of the new, *male-oriented* generation of gods, but also as Apollo the *purifier*. Indeed, the Aeschylean version of the story, essentially that of the poet Stesichorus (*ca.* 600 B.C.),[56] seems to have been closely associated with the popular rites of Apollo the Purifier [57]—and it is in this post-Homeric version that the killing of the mother first becomes central in the story.

Though I have so far spoken of two upsurges of this Oedipal-Orestean conflict in the normal male psychobiography, there are still further recurrences. Both clinical and theoretical work in recent decades make it evident that the pattern repeats itself in later life.[58–60] The intensity and the clinical significance of these recurrences depend on the success of the earlier resolutions. One such typical recurrence occurs in connection with parenthood. The parent's identification with his children, themselves undergoing the ordeal for the first time, evokes a resurgence of his own past Oedipal conflicts and characteristic Orestean response. There is little doubt that at still later climactic phases of life the task may again come to the fore, an old psychic wound having opened again under new stress.

This long period required to translate repression into sublimation, to purge the guilt, to turn outward to the world—all this may in everyday life be a battle fought again and again, on one battlefield and then another. In the *Oresteia* we see it as a single, long exile devoted to self-purification and to communal acceptance. The ideal outcome is then represented as a single decisive judgment issuing from an actual court proceeding in which gods and men participate. This trial constitutes the major portion of the last play in Aeschylus' trilogy. And this last play, too, expresses in truly remarkable ways certain crucial features of the psychological transformation at issue here.

In the final play, all the "forces" which have been at work at last come into the open, onto the stage; openly they make their pleas. Orestes has wandered "through seas and island cities, over the vast continent, wherever the earth's face is hard with wanderers' feet." [61] He has followed Apollo's injunction:

> *Keep courage firm; nurse your appointed pain. . . . Go to Athens, city of Pallas. . . . There I will set you judges; and with soothing pleas I, who first bade you take your mother's life, will bring from all your painful days final deliverance.*[62]

Freud gives this advice concerning the seeker after self-purgation and psychic liberation:

> He must find the courage to direct his attention to the phenomena of his illness. . . . If this new attitude toward the illness intensifies the conflicts and brings to the fore symptoms which till then had been indistinct, one can easily console the patient by pointing out that these are only necessary and temporary aggravations and that one cannot overcome an enemy who is absent or not within range.[63]

The "symptoms" and the forces behind them at last "come to the fore," to use Freud's phrase, in the great trial at Athens. The Furies, self-styled "black-robed daughters of ancient Night," appear from out of their "subterranean caverns of the blind." They come to claim their "ancient privilege none dares deny." That privilege is to enforce archaic laws of vengeance for blood crimes. With the coming of the Furies onstage, the archaic unconscious has at last come within the scope of the realistic ego and consciousness. It is the archaic mother image which is particularly in question.

From Olympus appears "bright Apollo" to plead his case before the court—*his* case because he pleads not only for Orestes but as the representative of the "younger gods who override the ancient laws." [64] Constantly emphasized in connection with Apollo is the intertwining of these themes of maleness, light, purification, and the coming of a new order. Apollo represents, psychologically, those primary, "ultimate" sources of energy and direction for the male ego, those psychic "givens" which dynamize its evolution specifically toward maleness, toward realism, and toward an adult integrity. We must never forget what Freud again and again emphasized: there *is* what he called the constitutional factor, and it is a fundamental one in psychic development. With the emergence of ego-psychology we have become more acutely aware that it is not only the primal unconscious which is a psychic "given"; the "civilizing" agencies of the psyche must be supposed to have their own primary energies and directedness.[65–68]

Athena also appears before us, the daughter and representative of Zeus and the organizer of the court. She is the appropriate one to have the decisive voice in this trial. She is the patron god of Athens and the goddess of reason. And although she is a woman, she is herself a synthesis of the male and female virtues; what is more, she here specifically represents the new order of male dominance:

> *No mother gave me birth. Therefore the father's claim in all things, save to give myself in marriage, wins my whole heart's loyalty.*[69]

When all claims have at last been made, it is Athena who will have heard all in a fair manner, who will "synthesize" the whole, render final judgment, and direct the execution of that judgment. In this she represents the highest order and most general functions of the ego: perceptual, synthetizing, judging, and executive.

Freud said:

> Analysis replaces the process of repression, which is an automatic and excessive one, by a temperate and purposeful control on the part of the highest mental faculties.[70]

The final play, *The Furies,* expresses in its psychological meaning this contrast between repression and reasonable control. It begins with the priestess of Apollo delivering a hymn to civilization, turning to open the curtain to the inner sanctum, and shrieking with horror as she beholds within

> *a fearful sight, appalling to describe. . . . There on the navel-stone . . . a man polluted . . . a strange company of women—no, not women; Gorgons . . . but these are wingless, black, utterly loathsome. . . .*[71]

And Apollo, in his way as "automatic and excessive" in his response to the Furies, cries out to the repulsive Furies:

> *Out of this temple! I command you, go at once! . . . Heaven loathes you. . . . Away!*[72]

By the end of this last play in the trilogy, however, all parties have been satisfied or appeased. Athena, the goddess of reason and Zeus' representative, quite accurately characterizes the new, reasonable spirit which has replaced harsh "repressive conflict":

> *Holy Persuasion too I bless, who softly strove with harsh denial, till Zeus the Pleader came to trial and crowned Persuasion with success.*[73]

What of the court itself? It is true Athena organizes this court, and when the jurors split their vote, hers is decisive. Still, the court itself is a human court. The jurors are Athenian citizens. The audience is Athenian. What is more, Athena announces to "citizens and jurors all" that this public trial is not to be a unique event. She calls for general recognition of

> *This court which I ordain today in perpetuity, that now and always justice may be well discerned.*[74]

All of this, of course, had luminous historical-political meaning for the Athenian audience, many of whom had lived through events here represented in mythic-poetic form. Our concern here, however, is as usual single-minded: we seek the psychological meaning. This, too, is sharp and clear. For when the realistic ego has at last mastered the archaic unconscious, when the preoccupation with inner conflict can therefore be abandoned, then the center of a man's existence is himself as a man among men, a man *of* the real world and not merely in it. Such a man is by no means insensitive to the daemonic, the divine, the sublime. On the contrary: a man of the world, in the sense here intended, is a man at last open to the world and to his fellow men as his fellows. And, although in a certain sense men's existence is the center, this does not imply, either in the play or in life, a denial of the marvelous, both holy and profane.

Orestes at last, then, emerges from obsessive horror, is done with arid exile and blood sacrifices. He comes into the bright clear air of Athens. There, in taking his place decisively among the community of men and linking his fate with theirs, he *sees* at last the realities from which before he merely suffered unseeing. In this vision his courage bears its fruit. And in this same vision we see how not only Orestes' fate but the order of gods and the communal destiny also are transformed.

For, when Orestes is declared free, this is not the result of some plain judgment based on the evidence. The fact is that there was a war of two radically opposed orders of existence. The old order, that represented by the archaic Furies, was duly established of old. The new order is that of the "young gods," those represented by Apollo, "bright" Apollo, the purifier. The dogmatic claims of the contending parties produce deadlock; and since there is no common ground for argument, the specious argumentation does not help. This state of affairs is reflected in an evenly split vote.

It is Athena's will which decides. In this sense the decision is "arbitrary." But her will operates now through the just procedures of the very court she has now established. And this is precisely the case in the reorganization of the psyche in overcoming the Oedipal conflicts. The new organization does not follow the "logic" of the old; its victory represents an ultimate psychic given, as has been mentioned earlier. The choice of the new solution, the Orestean solution is just that—a choice, a choice which does not follow from but which instead overturns the old psychic order. It both establishes and operates through the rational and realistic ego, the mind's "court" of judgment. This choice is our psychic destiny—though, like any destiny, we may evade it and pay the price of spiritual mortification.

Such a new order cannot be built upon total rejection of the old. The claims of the Furies are bona fide, and in some way the archaic females must be appeased. And it is this which is accomplished by Athena in precisely the way we should expect on the basis of the psychological analysis. Athena offers them a "bargain," a transformative bargain: if they will use their power to become the protectors of Athens, of the fertility of its families and of its lands, of hearth and of health, then they will be offered far greater honor and reverence than ever before. They will be no longer the Furies but the Gracious Ones, the "bright angels" of Eliot's *Family Reunion.* Athena assures them they will sit "on bright thrones in a holy cavern."[75] In this "sublimation" of their former status, they will still have ultimate access

ginal powers if stress and strain require: they
e "implacable and great Goddesses," [76] "dread
ly powers." [77] The transformation of the ar-
chaic mother image into the tender, de-sexualized, and protecting maternal image is effected.

After Athena's decision, Apollo and Orestes leave the stage. Orestes departs to take up his throne in Argos, now legitimate heir to Agamemnon, master of his fate. The Furies are appeased and civilized; Holy Persuasion is in command. For some time, almost without our realizing it, the Athenian court and community have been the "hero" of the play, Orestes the individual having faded into the background. (When inner conflict is resolved, the self as such ceases to occupy the center of the stage.) [78]

Now the city, the *polis*, dominates the stage at the end. The trilogy concludes triumphantly with a brilliant torchlight procession, all singing: gods, men, and fate are reconciled in this new order of existence brought into being through the resolute deeds and endurance of Orestes.

II

Henry Miller tells us that there is an old story of a man who committed fifty murders, then became conscience-stricken. He went to live for several years with a holy man, striving to reform his nature. At last he was sent into the world by his teacher, but he was still unsure. He wandered everywhere, did everything he could to purify himself. But the sign of his success did not come. One day he came upon a man attacking a woman. She cried piteously for help; the reformed murderer pleaded with the attacker to cease. But the attack was redoubled. At last the wanderer decided that though this were to renounce all hope of his own salvation, he could not stand by and see the woman murdered. He set upon the attacker and killed him. When he returned in despair to the holy man, the sign of his salvation had come. Henry Miller comments:

> There are murders and *murders* then. There is the kind that enslaves and the kind that liberates. But the final objective is to murder the murderer. The last act in the drama of "the ego and his own" is to murder one's own murderous self. To commit murder in full consciousness of the enormity of the crime is an act of liberation. It is heroic, and only those are capable of it who have purified their hearts of murder.[79]

Oedipus and Orestes murder. The crimes of Oedipus have their source in his murderous and lustful self. These are the crimes which ensnare, in the life of the psyche as well as in that of the tragic drama. The crimes of Orestes are the crimes which free; they murder the murderous self. To the infantile self, the Orestean deeds to be done appear as the deepest crime; for they will rupture the fabric of the old order of existence. But once these tasks are accomplished, one may say to oneself in retrospect, as Sartre's Orestes does: "that burden is my freedom." [80] Jean-Paul Sartre's Orestes, in *The Flies*, does refer to what he is going to do as "a crime," [81] but after it is done, he says:

> *I am no criminal, and you have no power to make me atone for an act I didn't regard as a crime.*[82]

Sartre, like Miller, emphasizes that what is necessary is that a man have "the courage of his crimes." [83]

Miller's story does not concern itself with the specific nature of the old order and of the new which emerges from it. And although Sartre uses the Orestes story, he, too, is unconcerned with the content of the new existence. He singles out for sole emphasis what we might here call the generic feature of the ego's triumphs. In mastering anxiety, whether it be the anxiety of the normal growth crises, neurotic anxiety, or the anxieties of a realistic adult facing his world, the ego must be prepared to abandon old object-cathexes and to risk new ones. What seemed the necessary foundations of existence must be shattered. "Mourning" there will be, but deepening of character, too, as a fruit of mourning. The ego must bear anxiety until a new order has been created, the old assimilated *in* the new.

This generic task of the ego, the mastery of anxiety, is at issue in the arts, philosophy, and religion of our time. It is the psychological meaning of the thesis that we must each commit a fateful deed, that we must have the courage of our "crime" if it is to be the kind which leads us into a new order of existence. The meaning and quality of this new order one cannot fully sense beforehand; we must wait and discover what destiny we ourselves have chosen. "Authentic existence" requires that we be ready to take the risk, have faith, but demand no guarantees. In psychoanalytic doctrine, there are analogous notions. I refer to the ego's capacity and will to bear the anxiety of facing infantile fantasy, to compare it with reality, to reject the domination of the fantasy, and, finally, to choose a new response rooted in reality. The earliest prototype of this achievement of liberation and self-mastery is the Orestean resolution of the Oedipal conflict.

The Aeschylean Orestes is thus a quite specific analogue of this central growth crisis. The specificity of the parallel in the Aeschylean Orestes story is at least as detailed as it is in the Oedipus story vis-à-vis the Oedipal conflict.

It is important to recall that such a prototypical situation is not merely temporally the first one of its kind. It is also a *model* upon which later responses build and out of which they evolve. The psychoanalytic notion of a genetic model has led to widespread misinterpretation. No one would say that the Beethoven *Eroica* symphony is a mere superficial variant on the Haydn symphonies, that it is "really" only a Haydn symphony. Yet none would deny that the former is modeled on and historically evolved from the latter. Analogously, there should be no ignoring of what is genuinely *new* in each ego-crisis in the course of life. But it is also important at times to detect the genetic model, the specific imagery and dynamics of the original Oedipal conflict and the Orestean resolution.

It could hardly be an accident that Aeschylus, who, in all probability, was most concerned to celebrate a political, social, religious rebirth, chose for his purposes the story of family intrigue that he did. Yet there is a *prima facie* paradox in choosing for such purposes the story of a murdered king and a faithless wife, of a young man who avenged his murdered father, murdered his mother and her paramour, and suffered in exile until he had purified himself. The very *prima facie* unlikeliness of the story as a medium for exhibiting a transformation of the divine as well as the earthly political order makes the psychological analysis presented here all the more plausible. For in terms of the psychological analysis we can see sharply those features of such an intra-family conflict which do have a systematic parallel to the patterns and the imagery on these other levels.

We can only list in a formula some of these patterns in the *Oresteia;* the reader of the plays must amplify for himself. Here are a few: the transition from the first dim fire in the darkness to the brilliant torch parade which at the end lights up the darkness; from the archaic order to the new and enlightened order; from the law of talion to the law of reason; from clan blood loyalties to individual responsibility and the community; from the female perversely like a male to the male order which allows the female a complementary role; from pre-Homeric Greece to the city-state of Athens; from the Eleusinian novice outside the temple to the initiate to whom the Eleusinian Mystery is revealed. All these transitions, and more, are vital elements in the *Oresteia.* They are not our business to discuss here. We need only note that all consist in a radically new synthesis of old materials, that the new synthesis is always a "civilizing" one. Most important and put most generally: all can and do stand as metaphors for each other; and the pattern which I have argued to be the psychological meaning of the *Oresteia* parallels in appropriate detail all of these. This psychological pattern was not, of course, constructed *ad hoc* as a parallel. It is a central pattern independently formulated and substantiated in the clinical-theoretical work of psychoanalysts.

It seems appropriate here to amplify a statement offered at the outset of this study. I believe it is due to the relatively late formulation and discussion of the theses of ego-psychology that such an early play as O'Neill's *Mourning Becomes Electra* (1929) treats the Orestes story primarily in terms of Oedipal conflict. Eliot (1939) has seen beyond this, as has Sartre (1942), though the one takes a religious and the other an atheistic stand. The latter two have seen farther in this connection than have a number of psychoanalytic writers still too preoccupied with the Oedipal references in the story.

Our view of the Orestes story provides us with a further and quite specific perspective upon a central contemporary predicament. Aeschylus' Orestes leaves for Argos, where he will carry on the family line and take up his royal role. By contrast, Sartre's Orestes, after having committed the killings, abandons Argos and is left wandering in exile, pursued by the Furies. The Greek Orestes had his established role to play, once free. Sartre's Orestes has—only freedom. His anguish is just beginning, for now he knows he is free to create an identity for himself, a world to inhabit. But he must create it out of nothing.

The contemporary emphasis on the "quest for identity" in psychological literature takes its place in the Orestes story exactly as it should. (And this is of course why Sartre in particular could use it as he did.) The Greek Orestes had only to solve the tasks set for him by Oedipus. The specific content of his future life was settled for him by the times and his place in them. The Golden Age was beginning when Aeschylus wrote: Greece had a form, a vision. Today, however, we must each of us live our Oedipal fate and take up our Orestean task—and then we have yet a final task, once free.

Each of us must build his own new Argos of th
realm. Each one must found a spiritual dyna
he knows may have no heirs. The superego and the ego
are today dynamic entities whose content often seems quite indeterminate for the psychically free man, the range of contemporary values and styles of life being so vast.

In our culture, which is conscious of all cultures and which constantly transcends its consciousness of itself, the psychological task of creating an identity may have *no general solution* so far as content goes. This is perhaps what it means to be genuinely *free*. The existentialists have insisted on this point.

Yet it may be that we overestimate our freedom with regard to the range of choices we have, the possibilities of new creation. Perhaps we are more like Orestes than we think. Our archaic family ties, our subjugation to the dwellers in the "subterranean caverns of the blind," and to the gods—all may be more unyielding than we would acknowledge. These may hold us to our individual fate or destiny the more irrevocably for being unacknowledged.

No doubt this question calls for an exploration which goes to the heart of the individual's existence. Our concern here, however, is the fact that this question, of such central contemporary concern, can be formulated and the alternatives defined within the framework of the Aeschylean story of Orestes. We look into the dark brilliance of its myriad facets; we see deep within a single nuclear form of life.

NOTES

1. E. O'Neill, *Mourning Becomes Electra* (1929, 1931), in *Three Plays of Eugene O'Neill* (New York: Vintage Books, n.d.).

2. T. S. Eliot, *The Family Reunion,* in *Complete Poems and Plays* (New York: Harcourt, Brace, 1950).

3. J. P. Sartre, *The Flies* (1943), in *No Exit and Three Other Plays* (New York: Vintage Books, 1955).

4. N. N. Dracoulides, "La généalogie des Atrides et l'aventure d'Oreste," *Psyche,* VII (1952), 805–817, and VIII (1953), 32–34. See also notes 5–9.

5. N. N. Dracoulides, "Profil psychoanalytique de Charles Baudelaire," *Psyche,* VIII (1953), 461–485.

6. J. Friedman and S. Gassel, "Orestes: A Psychoanalytic Approach to Dramatic Criticism, II," *Psychoanalytic Quarterly,* XX (1951), 423–433.

7. J. Friedman and S. Gassel, "Odysseus: The Return of the Primal Father," *Psychoanalytic Quarterly,* XXI (1952), 215–223.

8. J. T. MacCurdy, "Concerning Hamlet and Orestes," *Journal of Abnormal and Social Psychology,* XIII (1919), 250–260.

9. G. Roheim, "The Panic of the Gods," *Psychoanalytic Quarterly,* XXI (1952), 92–106.

10. Except where otherwise indicated, the quotations from Aeschylus are taken from the translation by Philip Vellacott (The Penguin Classics, L67, 1956). I have cited line numbers from the standard text rather than page numbers, since the latter vary from translation to translation, whereas the standard line numbers are almost always provided. Though I have quoted Vellacott's version for its poetic felicity, I have by no means relied on it for discovering the content and context of interpretation of the passages cited or of the plays as a whole. For these purposes, from among the many books and articles on the topic, I have relied mainly, though not exclusively, on the following (notes 11–25):

11. J. R. Bacon, "Three Notes on Aeschylus, *Prometheus Vinctus,*" *The Classical Review,* XLII (1928), 115–119.

12. J. H. Finley, *Pindar and Aeschylus* (Cambridge: Harvard University Press, 1955).

13. A. E. Haigh, *The Tragic Drama of the Greeks* (Oxford, 1896).

14. H. D. F. Kitto, *Form and Meaning in Drama* (New York: Barnes and Noble, 1960).

15. H. D. F. Kitto, *Greek Tragedy* (New York: Doubleday-Anchor, 1955).

16. R. Lattimore (trans.), *Aeschylus' Oresteia* (Chicago: University of Chicago Press, 1953).

17. D. W. Lucas, *The Greek Tragic Poets* (London: Cohen and West, 1950).

18. E. D. A. Morshead (trans.), *The House of Atreus* (Harvard Classics, n.d.).

19. M. H. Scharlemann, *The Influence of the Social Changes in Athens on the Development of Greek Tragedy* (Ph.D. dissertation, Washington University, 1938).

20. J. Sheppard, *Greek Tragedy* (Cambridge: Cambridge University Press, 1920).

21. W. B. Stanford, *Aeschylus in His Style* (Dublin: Dublin University Press, 1942).

22. G. Thomson, "Mystical Allusions in the Oresteia," *Journal of Hellenistic Studies,* LV (1935), 20–34.

23. G. Thomson, *The Oresteia of Aeschylus* (Vol. I: Greek and English texts; Vol. II: Commentary and appendices) (Cambridge: Cambridge University Press, 1938).

24. M. Tierney, "The Mysteries and the Oresteia," *Journal of Hellenistic Studies,* LVII (1937), 11–21.

25. T. G. Tucker, *The Choephori of Aeschylus* (Greek and English texts, with commentary, appendices) (Cambridge: Cambridge University Press, 1901).

26. Lines (henceforth: *ll.*) 298–304, *Choephori* (henceforth: *Cho.*).

27. *ll.* 454, 476–477, 481–483, 501–502, *Cho.*

28. *ll.* 4–5, *Cho.*

29. S. Freud, *The Ego and the Id,* in *The Standard Edition of the Complete Psychological Works of Sigmund Freud,* Vol. 19 (London: Hogarth Press, 1961), p. 34.

30. *ll.* 995–996, *Cho.*

31. *l.* 889, *Cho.* Cf. Thomson, *The Oresteia,* II, 234 (cited above, note 23).

32. *ll.* 895–897, *Cho.*

33. S. Freud, *An Outline of Psychoanalysis* (New York: W. W. Norton & Co., 1949), p. 89.

34. *Ibid.*, pp. 90, 94.
35. *Ibid.*, p. 99.
36. *l.* 898, *Cho.*
37. *ll.* 899–901, *Cho.*, and cf. Thomson's comment on these lines: Thomson, *The Oresteia,* Vol. II.
38. Freud, *The Ego and the Id,* p. 39.
39. Freud, *An Outline of Psychoanalysis,* p. 89.
40. *l.* 902, *Cho.*
41. Freud, *The Ego and the Id,* p. 39.
42. S. Freud, "Remembering, Repeating and Working Through," in *The Standard Edition of the Complete Psychological Works of Sigmund Freud,* Vol. 12 (London: Hogarth Press, 1958), p. 152.
43. S. Freud, *A General Introduction to Psychoanalysis* (New York: Garden City Press, 1943), p. 291.
44. *Ibid.*, p. 295.
45. *ll.* 545–548, *Cho.*
46. *ll.* 436–437, *Cho.*
47. *ll.* 237–239, Eumenides (henceforth: *Eum.*).
48. *ll.* 284–285, *Eum.*
49. *ll.* 237–239, *Eum.*
50. Freud, *The Ego and the Id,* p. 39.
51. *Loc. cit.*
52. *ll.* 280–289, *Eum.*
53. Freud, *The Ego and the Id,* Ch. 3.
54. P. Blos, *On Adolescence* (New York: The Free Press of Glencoe, 1962), p. 157.
55. *Ibid.*, p. 187.
56. Tucker, *The Choephori of Aeschylus,* p. xix.
57. *Ibid.*, pp. xxiii–xxiv.
58. See, for example, R. W. Coleman, E. Kris, and S. Provence, "The Study of Variations in Early Parental Attitudes," in *The Psychoanalytic Study of the Child,* Vol. 8 (New York: International Universities Press, 1953), pp. 20–47. See also notes 59 and 60.
59. H. Fingarette, *The Self in Transformation* (New York: Basic Books, 1963), Ch. 3.
60. E. Kris, "On Psychoanalysis and Education," *American Journal of Orthopsychiatry,* XVIII (1948), 622–635.
61. *ll.* 75–77, *Eum.*
62. *ll.* 78–84, *Eum.*
63. Freud, "Remembering, Repeating and Working Through," *loc. cit.*, p. 152.
64. For characteristic phrases as cited in this and the preceding paragraph, cf. *ll.* 298–399, 747–748, 781–795, *Eum.*

65. S. Freud, "Analysis Terminable and Interminable," in *Collected Papers,* Vol. 5 (New York: Basic Books, 1959), pp. 343–344.

66. H. Hartmann, *Ego Psychology and the Problem of Adaptation* (New York: International Universities Press, 1958).

67. H. Hartmann, "Notes on the Reality Principle," in *The Psychoanalytic Study of the Child,* Vol. II (1956).

68. H. Hartmann, E. Kris, and R. M. Loewenstein: see the series of papers by these authors collectively and separately in *ibid.,* Vols. 1, 2, 3, 5, 7.

69. *ll.* 739–741, *Eum.*

70. S. Freud, "Analysis of a Phobia in a Five-Year-Old Boy," *Collected Papers,* Vol. 3, p. 285.

71. *ll.* 34–51, *Eum.*

72. *ll.* 179–197, *Eum.*

73. *ll.* 971–975, *Eum.*

74. *ll.* 572–576, *Eum.*

75. *ll.* 809–810, *Eum.*

76. *ll.* 929–930, *Eum.*

77. *ll.* 1033–1034, *Eum.*

78. Cf. Fingarette, *op. cit.,* Ch. 7.

79. H. Miller, "Murder the Murderer," in *Remember to Remember* (New York: New Directions, 1947).

80. Sartre, *op. cit.,* p. 108.

81. *Ibid.,* p. 63.

82. *Ibid.,* p. 116.

83. *Ibid.,* p. 126.

6 / *The Good Samaritan and the Law*

Over two thousand years ago the great Chinese philosopher Mencius said: "All men have a capacity for compassion." Mencius said: "My meaning may be illustrated thus: . . . if men see a child about to fall into a well, they will without exception experience a feeling of alarm and distress. This is not because they know the child's parents, nor out of a desire for praise by neighbors and friends, nor out of dislike for the bad reputation that would ensue if they did not go to the rescue. From this we may conclude that without compassion one would not be a human being."

There is no doubt Mencius was right—as far as he

went. Yet, as I thought of this text from ancient China, I could not help but think also of the experience two of my colleagues had a while ago. They were hurrying to a meeting in a relatively strange part of town. Suddenly, from out of a nearby apartment-house window, a woman began crying for help. My friends were of course startled and frightened. They debated for a few moments whether to go their way or rush to the rescue. The screams continued. The impulse to keep on their way was strong; but they finally decided to go into the house. As they rushed up several flights of stairs, they passed a number of apartment dwellers, standing in the hall at their open doors, listening avidly to the increasingly anguished screams. Frightened and breathless, my friends at last arrived and banged on the door. To their utter amazement, the woman herself opened it. It was immediately obvious that the well-meaning Samaritans had interrupted a glorious family fight. The woman proceeded to deliver a rapid-fire, full-voice lecture on a citizen's right to privacy, on the obnoxiousness of self-appointed Good Samaritans, and on her own good nature which prevented her from reporting the intruders to the police.

Such are some of the real-life complications faced by the Samaritan. These practical situations raise three different sorts of critical questions. First, there are the objective factual questions: What is going on? What can be done? What is the cost of doing it? The newspaper reader, in the quiet of his home and well after the fact, thinks he knows the facts, and it seems obvious to him what should have been done. But things are often not so simple to the man on the spot. I must leave the discussion of such important questions to those who are expert in problems of police and other rescue tasks.

The second sort of critical question has to do with the often conflicting impulses and emotions which the potential Good Samaritan may find in his breast. One might think of these as factual questions, too, but questions, perhaps, of psychological or subjective fact. They, too, are complex. We know that the compassionate impulses are not the only common ones. There is also the impulse to stand and stare—incidentally disrupting bona fide rescue attempts as often as not. There are also the latent sadistic impulses—not infrequently the onlookers join in the aggression. There is commonly fear and repugnance before anyone who is odd, helpless, suffering, or attacked. Such emotions often evoke a powerful impulse simply to get away as fast as possible. What is the inner structure of these emotions and impulses and what is their strength? What are their causes, their consequences, their role in the psychic economy and in the social process? These very critical questions fall most directly in the field of the psychiatrist and the social scientist rather than in that of the philosopher.

Since we are not merely the victims of our impulses and beliefs, there is still a third critical set of questions: In the light of our beliefs and our impulses, what would be the *best* thing to do, what *ought* I to do? And finally, what do I actually *decide* to do? Such questions are, broadly speaking, the moral and decisional questions.

It may be relevant to note that some psychiatrists or sociologists may deny that this last set of questions is genuinely independent and basic. They may have no place in their theories or equations for moral principles above causality; they may have no place for free choice. For them the question what *ought* I to do may be considered only a symptom of one more psychological force: the impulse to follow some such rule as "help others." They will then conceive of this impulse as having a greater or lesser magnitude, balancing off to some extent the contrary impulses. My action will still be conceived by them, at least in theory, as a mathematically calculable one rather than a free choice.

However, those who must think in terms of law cannot take moral and decisional questions to be a mere subclass of factual questions about causes or forces, whether objective *or* subjective. In law, one must view choice and moral responsibility as fundamental, irreducible categories. What is more, the layman who is the Samaritan in an actual crisis situation *cannot*—I emphasize *cannot* —think of his action as causally necessitated. Imagine the person on the spot saying to himself: "Since my act is the mathematical resultant of the strength of my desires, and since in any case I can't objectively measure my desires, the best thing for *me* to do is to wait to see what I *do* do." Even in this absurd case, the person is *deciding* to wait and see.

These moral and decisional questions then are fundamental, irreducible to factual questions. And so I turn to moral obligation as one basis for decision.

My first proposition is that we do acknowledge that there *is* some obligation to help a person in distress. This has been assumed by speakers today, but it can be briefly shown in the following ways: A person who comes upon a stranger in trouble may be frightened or repelled and inclined to give in to these feelings; but unless he is literally panicked, he will try to justify giving in. He may say to himself: "It's none of my business—I don't know what's behind this; I might even aggravate the injury; there might be trouble later for me or for my family; besides I'm late for my appointment; anyway, why should *I* be the one to stop? Maybe someone else has already gone for help."

Such an inner debate would be pointless if it were not for a *tacit initial assumption* which might be phrased this way: "If a person is in great distress, and if I am the one available to help, then, all else being equal, I *do* have some obligation to help." Only because one tacitly assumes such an obligation does it make sense to run through all the *contrary* obligations and inconveniences in order to justify *not* helping. Sometimes we avoid obvious inner debate by pretending not to notice the person's distress—but this pretense itself reveals our tacit acknowledgment that, if we *do* notice, we *are* under some obligation.

The real problems the Samaritan, then, faces are not such generalities as: "Do I ever have a free choice?" Or, "Am I in *any* way obligated to help?" Nor do I think the problem is simply a lack of the willingness to carry out the obligation. No doubt we can always do with more good will than exists in this imperfect world. But even the man of good will faces serious problems here. In the practical context, he faces the perplexing questions: "How shall I weigh this obligation-to-help along with *other conflicting* obligations; how shall I weigh it in the light of my conflicting impulses; how shall I weigh it in the light of my objective uncertainty about what is going on here? In short, how can I put specific content into it?"

Now one might argue that the obligation to be neighborly is general rather than specific because it is meant as a moral absolute. As such, this obligation would have priority in *every* way over every other consideration. As such, it would be a counsel of perfection, a complete dedication of our existence to this principle. But most of us know we are not, will not be perfect. We do not live by absolutes. We are only everyday, garden-variety Samaritans.

Suppose we look then to the classical sources in which this obligation-to-help-the-stranger is presented to us; perhaps the context, language, and imagery of the classical sources will provide the clues we need to the specific scope and force of the obligation in practical life.

The first and most obvious classical source for our purposes is clear enough; it is the Gospel story of the Samaritan. It deserves a slightly more detailed attention in my remarks than it has yet been given.

This story in Luke, Chapter 10, is simple enough. Jesus is questioned by a lawyer who asks what is necessary to inherit eternal life. When Jesus asks him what the law on the matter is, it turns out the lawyer can recite the law perfectly, but—the nature of lawyers being apparently everywhere the same—he wants to argue the interpretation of one of the words in it.

The law is this: "Love the Lord thy God with all thy heart and with all thy soul and with all thy strength; and thy neighbor as thyself." The lawyer wants to know: "Who *is* my neighbor?" Whereupon Jesus tells the story of the Samaritan. A man is going along the road from Jerusalem to Jericho when he is set upon by thieves, who strip him and beat him, leaving him for dead. A priest who is going along the road sees him, but passes by on the other side. A Levite, that is to say, a man from one of the quasi-priestly castes, does the same. But a certain Samaritan stops. The Samaritan binds up the poor man's wounds, helps him to a place of refuge at an inn, asks the innkeeper to take good care of the man, gives the innkeeper some money, and assures the innkeeper that if the expenses turn out to be more, the rest will be forthcoming when the Samaritan returns on his way back.

That is the story; and Jesus asks the lawyer: "Which one of the three was the neighbor to the victim?" The lawyer gives the obvious answer—the Samaritan. "Go and do thou likewise," says Jesus.

This story, like many traditional stories at the time, turns upon the differing responses of priest, Levite, and layman. But, typically in such stories, the layman as well as the other two would be Jews. Jesus, however, substitutes a Samaritan, a geographical neighbor but one who was despised and hated by the Jews of the time as being uncouth, unclean, immoral, and heretical. Thus the story as told by Jesus was intended to teach most emphatically that love of neighbor is so universal, so unqualified a principle as to include even the meanest of men being neighbor to the most self-righteous of enemies. The Gospel source also emphasizes *acting* as a neighbor, *decision* rather than legalistic classification. Finally, and of highest importance, the story has to do with eternal life, personal salvation—not with problems of keeping the public order.

When I say that this parable is concerned with the ultimate question of personal salvation through personal decision and unqualified commitment, I have in mind the other side of the coin: whether my soul is saved or not is none of the state's business. Let Caesar regulate his own affairs: keeping the public order and the public well-being. My soul is *my* affair. This was Jesus' teaching; it is also central to our own political tradition.

Let me recall for a moment the main thread of my

argument. I have dwelt at some little length upon the parable of the Good Samaritan since it is a classic source par excellence in our own tradition, and as such it might help to put specific content into the obligation of the citizen. However, as we now see, it turns out that the emphasis in the Gospel context is not on practical questions but on the inward and eternal life, commitment and salvation.

If we look to other classical sources for an analogous teaching of neighborly love, we find it indeed. The Old Testament teaches love of neighbor in the Book of Leviticus. The theme of helping one's fellow being is also central in Mahayana Buddhism and in the teaching of Confucius, a remarkable fact in view of the great gaps —philosophical, geographical, and cultural—which otherwise separate these teachings from those of Biblical lands. But here again the teaching is in each case a religious, salvationist one, or a counsel of ultimate human perfection.

The moral of the Good Samaritan parable is not limited to the classical religious sources, however. We can, if we wish, translate it into more general terms, without committing ourselves to supernaturalistic doctrines of the soul, of salvation, or of Heaven or Hell. One such account would consist in seeing that the question, "Shall I help this stranger in his dire need?" is inextricably connected with the question: "What kind of person am I?"—or, more precisely, "What kind of person *shall* I be?"—or, still more precisely yet: "What shall I *make* of myself?" These are truly questions of one's personal salvation or damnation, whether we take these terms in a specific theological sense or not.

It is conceivable that a person might live a terribly rigid and narrow life in which the Samaritan question never comes up in an urgent way; and such a person might be neutral on the issue. *But*—once the occasion does arise, a person cannot be neutral; the issue is forced. Then one must either decide to help the stranger or decide to reject his cry for help. Whichever way one decides, one has been forced to take a stand—and thus to make oneself into a different kind of person from what one was before, perhaps a nobler person, perhaps a meaner person. One's stand toward the Other reflects one's stand toward oneself.

For those who prefer evidence from contemporary sources, I suggest, among a number one might think of, Albert Camus' novel *The Fall*. In this remarkable narrative, Camus shows us the inside story of how the failure to come to a stranger's aid turns out to be only the objective symbol of a life which is an inward mockery of itself. The central figure—incidentally, he is a lawyer—is first called to himself by his failure to save another human being from death; this failure soon reveals itself to him as only the outward expression of a constant but *covert* betrayal of others; and this constant betrayal of *others* he discovers to be only an aspect of an inward *self*-betrayal. Camus presents and justifies his narrative in human terms, but he explicitly connects it with the traditional religious teaching of damnation and salvation: the lawyer's living Hell is presented symbolically as Dante's inner circle of Hell.

Having briefly noted how remarkable a consensus among varied sources can be found, I now only wish to note that the consensus includes the point that this teaching goes to the very heart of one's personal existence, that it is indeed, and in a word, a teaching of salvation, whether secular or religious. Therefore, if I were a Samaritan, as I see it I could take one of two attitudes. One attitude is to look at what I am about to do—or perhaps already have done—as a matter of profoundly personal decision, a matter between me and my conscience or me and my God, as relevant to my own spiritual life or death. There is really nothing more to be *said* here; what is needed is a personal *decision.* And *that,* it seems to me, is the end of that topic. I think it is an error, an obstacle to progress, to base community legal action on this spiritual and personal basis.

There is, however, another attitude I may take. I may put aside the perspective of salvation. I may turn instead to an attempt to understand my obligations in the context of good citizenship, of modest decency rather than ultimate Virtue, of everyday reasonableness rather than "Reason" with a capital "R."

Then the community and its more mundane concerns

become relevant. Somewhere, somehow, in the nature of the community we may find the clue to the good citizen's version of the obligation to rescue the stranger. And here, I believe, we do in fact get a clue as to how to produce an answer.

A community is not merely a miscellaneous collection of specific regulations, laws, institutions. Its foundation is in the acknowledgment by its members that there *is* a community, that the members of the community are committed to one another to make some sacrifices of their energies, their wealth, their comfort for the sake of preserving the integrity of the community and enjoying its rewards. In our own case, we are committed to a community which aims to assure to its members a right to life, liberty, and the pursuit of happiness. If we think in these terms, then, it seems to me, there is implied a general acknowledgment of some fundamental and at least minimal obligation to make sacrifices for the sake of public order and the safety of those who belong in the community. This *general* obligation underlies and justifies the specific obligations spelled out in law and custom.

For example, we are generally obligated to respect life and property when we drive a car. But it is not enough to tell drivers that they are obligated to drive safely; we must have *rules* of the road and *customs* of the road. Of course, always in force and underlying these there remains the general obligation to drive safely. The specific rules and customs give guidance as to the meaning of this general obligation in the common driving situations where otherwise legitimate doubt and conflict might reign. Again, we don't merely ask in general that citizens be loyal—we spell out military-service laws, laws defining treason, rules for security classification of documents, pledges of allegiance, and so on. We do not merely ask citizens to have a care for the public health—we spell out public health and safety laws. We do not merely ask that all contribute generously to financing government—we have tax laws. Not everything is in law or regulation, of course; a great deal is left to custom—customs of etiquette, of respect for personal privacy, of good faith in various transactions. The general principles of loyalty, health, safety, courtesy, mutual respect remain essential—not only as the justification for custom and rule but also because there are always gray areas and new problems where the custom and rule or law don't quite apply. Even in these borderline areas we often get a useful cue by comparing the doubtful case with the closest parallel cases where law or custom *is* specific. Finally, should one of these gray areas seem sufficiently troublesome, we may spell out new rules or laws, or revise the old, so as to cover the problem explicitly.

In this way, custom and explicit rule provide us with a more or less detailed map of areas which are only broadly delimited by our general communal obligation.

This map orients us, even if it does not always directly answer our every question.

If we grant that there is a general communal obligation to help keep the public order and protect the lives and property of the citizenry, what is the case specifically with respect to the person who comes upon a stranger in dire straits? Is our general obligation adequately spelled out in custom or in law?

I am not sure about the current custom. It may be, as our newspapers and police officers suggest, that there really are fewer Good Samaritans today than in earlier generations. Perhaps once there was a custom, and perhaps it is rapidly disappearing. It may be, however, that there only *seem* to be fewer Good Samaritans because our moral demands have increased. After all, a single killing in the South shocks our moral conscience today, whereas a generation or so ago lynchings were *more* common but *less* noticed. I am not so sure that things have not got relatively worse in the recent short run. In any case, this question as to what is really happening to our customs and group values, and why it is happening, is a historical-sociological question of the first importance. As such, it is in the province of the social scientists. But, in any case, I can speak for myself as a potential Samaritan. As far as custom goes, I am not sure what custom is, or was. Is it customary to rush to the aid of the injured or attacked? Or does one customarily run for a policeman or at least a telephone, letting the sufferer manage as best he can? If one has grounds to fear great financial liability, public embarrassment, or even mortal danger, does one intervene at all?—what is the custom here? I frankly don't know what the actual custom is. I suspect it varies with the circumstances and the individuals—in short, I suspect there is no custom but a complete range of all the possible responses.

In any case, whatever used to be the custom, it is evident that nowadays there is concern and confusion in our *minds*. Therefore, *I* cannot look to custom as a guide to my specific obligations in the practical emergency situations I am likely to meet.

In the absence of clear custom, it would seem to me that explicit public policy—as expressed in law and regulation—would be of the essence if we are to have practical guidance about the Samaritan's obligation. But here, I gather, the law provides no guide. Yet this *is* the community's business. This is the way it normally carries on its business. The precise formulation of such law is no doubt a subtle and complex affair. However, I know of no insuperable difficulties in the way of doing it, and we have learned how these difficulties are overcome in Europe. From a moral standpoint—and this is my primary concern here—I think a body of specific law or regulations is essential. It is the only alternative to editorializing platitudes and generalities which substitute the thrill of righteous indignation, and the fascination with scandal, for substantive clarification of genuine confusion.

The law should encourage coming to another's aid by providing legitimate physical, financial, and legal protection; the law should lessen the temptation to avoid bringing aid by providing penalties. Concrete suggestions for such measures have already been forthcoming. In this way, law, and of course other public regulations, can also define in detail and express the public attitude on these issues. The law *can* help shape social attitudes and actions.

I do not mean to claim that this line of action will solve the problem. I have bypassed the sociological, anthropological, psychiatric, and political problems. The *total* problem of the Samaritan involves all these areas. But the *moral* problem of the Samaritan is the one I have been concerned with. It is only one aspect, though an important one.

I have one brief qualification to make. Most of what I have said is based on the supposition that the Good Samaritan problem *is* a significant social problem. But it may be that in fact it is not a major social problem except insofar as newspaper sensationalism has made it such. I do not know. If it should be a problem of newspaper sensationalism rather than a problem of increasing public callousness or confusion and fear, then we might do better to let the law alone.

7 / Human Community as Holy Rite: An Interpretation of Confucius' Analects

This essay is aimed at revealing the magic power which Confucius saw, quite correctly, as the very essence of human virtue. And it is finally by way of the magical that we can also arrive at the best vantage point for seeing the holiness in human existence which Confucius saw as central. In the twentieth century, this central role of the holy in Confucius' teaching has been largely ignored because we have failed to grasp the existential point of that teaching.

Specifically, what is needed (and is here proposed) is a reinterpretation which makes use of contemporary philosophical understanding. And in fact such a reinterpretation casts, by reflection as it were, illumination into dimensions of our own philosophical thought which have remained in shadow.

The distinctive philosophical insight in the *Analects*, or at least in its more authentic "core," was quickly obscured as the ideas of rival schools infected Confucius' teaching.[1] And it is not surprising that this insight, requiring as it does a certain emphasis on the magical and religious dimensions of the *Analects*, is absent from the usual Western-influenced interpretations of modern times. Today the *Analects* is read, in its main drift, as an empirical, humanist, this-worldly teaching, or as a parallel to Platonist-rationalist doctrines. Indeed, the teaching of the *Analects* is often viewed as a major step toward the explicit rejection of superstition or heavy reliance on "supernatural forces."[2]

There is no doubt that the world of the *Analects* is profoundly different in its quality from that of Moses, Aeschylus, Jesus, Gautama Buddha, Lao-tse, or the Upanishadic teachers. In certain obvious respects, the *Analects* does indeed represent the world of a humanist and a traditionalist, one who is, however, sufficiently traditional to render a kind of pragmatic homage, when necessary, to the spirits.

"Devote yourself to man's duties," says the Master; "respect spiritual beings but keep distance" (6:20).[3] He suited the deed to the precept and himself "never talked of prodigies, feats of strength, disorders, or spirits" (7:20). In response to direct questions about the transcendental and supernatural, he said: "Until you are able to serve men, how can you serve spiritual beings? Until you know about life, how can you know about death?" (11:11).

If we examine the substance of the *Analects* text, it is quickly evident that the topics and the chief concepts pertain primarily to our human nature, comportment, and relationships. Merely to list some of the constantly recurring themes suffices for our present purposes: Rite (*Li*), Humaneness (*Jen*), Reciprocity (*Shu*), Loyalty (*Chung*), Learning (*Hsueh*), Music (*Le*), and the concepts by which are defined the familial-social relationships and obligations (prince, father, and so on).

The this-worldly, practical humanism of the *Analects* is further deepened by the teaching that the moral and spiritual achievements of man do not depend on tricks or luck, or on esoteric spells, or on any purely external agency. One's spiritual condition depends on the "stuff" one has to begin with, on the amount and quality of study and good hard work one puts into "shaping" it. Spiritual nobility calls for persistence and effort. "First the difficult . . ." (6:20). "His burden is heavy and his course is long. He has taken *jen* as his burden—is that not heavy?" (8:7). What disquieted Confucius was "leaving virtue untended and learning unperfected, hearing about what is right but not managing either to turn toward it or to reform what is evil" (7:3). The disciple of Confucius was surely all too aware that his task was one calling not for amazement and miracle but for constant "cutting, filing, carving, polishing" (1:15) in order to become a fully and truly human being, a worthy participant in society. All this seems the very essence of the anti-magical in outlook. Nor does it have the aura of the Divine.

Yet, in spite of this dedicated and apparently secular prosaic moralism, we also find occasional comments in the *Analects* which seem to reveal a belief in magical powers of profound importance. By "magic" I mean the power of a specific person to accomplish his will directly and effortlessly through ritual gesture and incantation. The user of magic does not work by strategies and devices as means toward an end; he does not use coercion or physical forces. There are no pragmatically developed and tested strategies or tactics. He simply wills the end in the proper ritual setting and with the proper ritual gesture and word; without further effort on his part, the deed is accomplished. Confucius' words at times strongly suggest some fundamental magical power as central to this way. (In the following citations, the Chinese terms all are central to Confucius' thought, and they designate powers, states, and forms of action of fundamental value. Insofar as necessary, they will be discussed later.)

"Is *jen* far away? As soon as I want it, it is here" (7:29).

"If a man for one day subdue himself and return to *li*, everyone in the world will respond to his *jen*" (12:1).

Shun, the great sage-ruler, "merely placed himself gravely and reverently with his face due south (the ruler's ritual posture); that was all" (i.e., and the affairs of his reign proceeded without flaw) (15:4).

The magical element always involves great effects produced effortlessly, marvelously, with an irresistible power that is itself intangible, invisible, unmanifest. "With correct comportment, no commands are necessary, yet affairs proceed" (13:6). "The character of a noble man is like wind, that of ordinary men like grass; when the wind blows the grass must bend" (12:19). "To govern by *te* is to be like the North Polar Star; it remains in place while all the other stars revolve in homage about it" (2:1).

Such comments can be taken in various ways. One may simply note that, as Duyvendak remarks, the "original magical meaning" of 12:1 is "unmistakable," or that the ritual posture of Shun in 15:4 is "a state of the highest magical potency." [4] In short, one may admit that these are genuine residues of "superstition" in the *Analects*.

However, many modern interpreters of the *Analects* have wished to read Confucius more "sympathetically," that is, as one whose philosophical claims would have maximum validity for us in our own familiar and accepted terms. In order to do this, these commentators have generally tried to minimize to the irreducible the magical claims in the *Analects*. For it is accepted as an axiom in our times that the goal of direct action by incantation and ritual gesture cannot be taken as a serious possibility. (The important exception to this general acceptance of the axiom, to be discussed later, is contemporary "linguistic analysis." But the import of this work has as yet hardly extended beyond the world of professional philosophy.)

The suggestion of magic and marvel so uncongenial to the contemporary taste may be dissipated in various ways: only one of the sayings I have quoted comes from the portion of the *Analects*—Books 3 to 8—which has been most widely of all accepted as "authentic" in the main. The other sayings might be among the many interpolations, often alien in spirit to Confucius, which are known to be in the received text. Or one might hold that the magical element is quite restricted in scope, applying only to the ruler, or even the perfect ruler alone.[5] Still another possible method of "interpreting away" the "magical" statements is to suppose that Confucius was merely emphasizing and dramatizing the otherwise familiar power of setting a good example.[6] In short, on this view we must take the "magical" sayings as being poetic statements of a prosaic truth. Finally, one might simply argue that Confucius was not consistent on the issue—perhaps that he was mainly and characteristically anti-magic, but, as might well be expected, he had not entirely freed himself of deep-rooted traditional beliefs.

All of these interpretations take the teaching of a magical dimension to human virtue as an *obstacle* to acceptance by the sophisticated citizen of the twentieth century. The magic must be interpreted away or else treated as a historically understandable failure on Confucius' part. I prefer to think we can still learn from Confucius on this issue if we do not begin by supposing the obvious meaning of his words to be unacceptable.

Rather than engage in polemics regarding these other interpretations, I shall devote the remainder of this essay to a positive exposition of what I take to be the genuine and sound magical view of man in Confucius' teaching. I do not hold that my interpretation is correct to the exclusion of all others. There is no reason to suppose that an innovator such as Confucius distinguishes all possible meanings of what he says and consciously intends only one of these meanings to the exclusion of all others. One should assume the contrary. Of the various meanings of the Confucian magical teaching, I believe the one to be elaborated in the following remarks is authentic, central, and still unappreciated.

Confucius saw, and tried to call to our attention, that the truly, distinctively human powers have, characteristically, a magical quality. His task, therefore, required, in effect, that he reveal what is already so familiar and universal as to be unnoticed. What is necessary in such cases is that one come upon this "obvious" dimension of our existence in a new way, in the right way. Where can one find such a new path to this familiar area, one which provides a new and revealing perspective? Confucius found the path: we go by way of the notion of *li*.

One has to labor long and hard to learn *li*. The word in its root meaning is close to "holy ritual," "sacred ceremony." But characteristic of Confucius' teaching is the use of the language and imagery of *li* as a medium within which to talk about the entire body of the *mores*, or more precisely, of the authentic tradition and reasonable conventions of society.[7] Confucius taught that the ability to act according to *li* and the will to submit to *li* are essential to that perfect and peculiarly human virtue or power which can be man's. Confucius thus does two things here: he calls our attention to the entire body of tradition and convention, and he calls upon us to see all this by means of a metaphor, through the imagery of sacred ceremony, holy rite.

The (spiritually) noble man is one who has labored at the alchemy of fusing social forms (*li*) and raw personal existence in such a way as to transmute them into a way of being which realizes *te*, the distinctively human virtue or power.

Te is realized in concrete acts of human intercourse, the acts being *of* a pattern. These patterns have certain general features, features common to all such patterns of *li:* they are all expressive of "man-to-man-ness," of reciprocal loyalty and respect. But the patterns are also specific: they differentiate and they define in detail the ritual performance-repertoires which constitute civilized, i.e., truly human, patterns of mourning, marrying, and fighting, of being a prince, a father, a son, and so on. However, men are by no means conceived as being mere standardized units mechanically carrying out prescribed routines in the service of some Cosmic or Social Law. Nor are they self-sufficient individual souls who happen to consent to a Social Contract. Men become truly human as their raw impulse is shaped by *li.* And *li* is the fulfillment of human impulse, the civilized expression of it—not a formalistic dehumanization. *Li* is the specifically humanizing form of the dynamic relation of man-to-man.

The novel and creative insight of Confucius was to see this aspect of human existence, its form as learned tradition and convention, in terms of a particular revelatory image: *li,* i.e., "holy rite," "sacred ceremony," in the usual meaning of the term prior to Confucius.

In well-learned ceremony, each person does what he is supposed to do according to a pattern. My gestures are coordinated harmoniously with yours—though neither of us has to force, push, demand, compel, or otherwise "make" this happen. Our gestures are in turn smoothly followed by those of the other participants, all equally effortlessly. If we all "submit" to the ceremony, then all that is needed—quite literally—is the initial ritual gesture in the proper ceremonial context; from there onward everything "happens." What action did Shun (the sage-ruler) take? "He merely placed himself gravely and reverently with his face due south; that was all" (15:4). Let us consider in at least a little detail the distinctive features of action emphasized by this revelatory image of Holy Rite.

It is important that we do not think of this effortlessness as "mechanical" or "automatic." If it is so, then, as Confucius repeatedly indicates, the ceremony is dead, sterile, empty: there is no *spirit* in it. The truly ceremonial "takes place"; there is a kind of spontaneity. It happens "of itself." There is life in it because the individuals do it with inner seriousness and sincere feeling. For ceremony to be authentic, one must "participate in the sacrifice"; otherwise it is as if one "did not sacrifice at all" (3:12). To put it another way, there are two contrasting kinds of failure in carrying out *li:* the ceremony may be awkwardly performed for lack of learning and skill; or the ceremony may have a surface slickness but yet be dull, mechanical, for lack of serious purpose and commitment. Beautiful and effective ceremony requires the personal "presence" to be fused with learned ceremonial skill. This ideal fusion is true *li* as sacred rite.

Confucius characteristically and sharply contrasts the

ruler who uses *li* with the ruler who seeks to attain his ends by means of commands, threats, regulations, punishments, and force (2:3). The force of coercion is manifest and tangible, whereas the vast (and sacred) forces at work in *li* are invisible and intangible. *Li* works through spontaneous coordination rooted in reverent dignity. The perfection in Holy Rite is esthetic as well as spiritual.

Having considered holy ceremony in itself, we are now prepared to turn to more everyday aspects of life. This is in effect what Confucius invites us to do; it is the foundation for his perspective on man.

I see you on the street; I smile, walk toward you, put out my hand to shake yours. And behold!—without any command, stratagem, force, special tricks or tools, without any effort on my part to make you do so, you spontaneously turn toward me, return my smile, raise your hand toward mine. We shake hands—not by my pulling your hand up and down or your pulling mine, but by spontaneous and perfect cooperative action. Normally we do not notice the subtlety and amazing complexity of this coordinated "ritual" act. This subtlety and complexity become very evident, however, if one has had to learn the ceremony only from a book of instructions, or if one is a foreigner from a non-handshaking culture.

Nor normally do we notice that the "ritual" has "life" in it, that we are "present" to each other, at least to some minimal extent. As Confucius said, there are always the general and fundamental requirements of reciprocal good faith and respect. This mutual respect is not the same as a conscious feeling of mutual respect; when I am *aware* of a respect for you, I am much more likely to be piously fatuous or perhaps self-consciously embarrassed; and no doubt our little "ceremony" will reveal this in certain awkwardnesses. (I put out my hand too soon and am left with it hanging in mid-air.) No, the authenticity of the mutual respect does not require that I consciously feel respect or focus my attention on my respect for you; it is fully expressed in the correct, "live," and spontaneous performance of the *act*. Just as an aerial acrobat must, at least for the purposes at hand, possess (but not think about his) complete trust in his partner if the trick is to come off, so we who shake hands, though the stakes are less, must have (but not think about) respect and trust. Otherwise we find ourselves fumbling awkwardly or performing in a lifeless fashion which easily conveys its meaninglessness to the other.

Clearly it is not necessary that our reciprocal respect and good faith go very far in order for us to accomplish a reasonably successful handshake and greeting. Yet even here, the sensitive person can often plumb the depths of another's attitude from a handshake. This depth of human relationship expressible in a "ceremonial" gesture is in good part possible because of the remarkable specificity of the ceremony. For example, if I am your former teacher, you will spontaneously be rather obvious in walking toward me rather than waiting for me to walk toward you. You will allow a certain subtle reserve in your handshake, even though it will be warm. You will not slap me on the back, though conceivably I might grasp you by the shoulder with my free hand. There are indescribably many subtleties in the distinctions, nuances, and minute but meaningful variations in gesture. If we do try to describe these subtle variations and their rules, we immediately sound like Book 10 of the *Analects*, whose ceremonial recipes initially seem to the modern American reader to be the quintessence of quaint and extreme traditionalism. It is in just such ways that social activity is coordinated in civilized society, without effort or planning, but simply by spontaneously initiating the appropriate ritual gesture in an appropriate setting. This power of *li*, Confucius says, depends upon prior learning. It is not inborn.

The effortless power of *li* can also be used to accomplish physical ends, though we usually do not think of it this way. Let us suppose I wish to bring a book from my office to my classroom. If I have no magic powers, I must literally take steps—walk to my office, push the door open, lift the book with my own muscles, physically carry it back. But there is also magic—the proper ritual expression of my wish which will accomplish my wish with no such effort on my part. I turn politely, i.e., ceremonially, to one of my students in class and merely express in an appropriate and polite (ritual) formula my wish that he bring me the book. This proper ceremonial expression of my wish is all; I do not need to force him, threaten him, trick him. I do not need to do anything more myself. In almost no time the book is in my hands, as I wished! This is a uniquely human way of getting things done.

The examples of handshaking and of making a request are humble; the moral is profound. These complex but familiar gestures are characteristic of human relationships at their most human: we are least like anything else in the world when we do not treat each other as physical objects, as animals, or even as subhuman creatures to be driven, threatened, forced, maneuvered. Looking at these "ceremonies" through the image of *li*, we realize that explicitly sacred rite can be seen as an emphatic, intensified, and sharply elaborated extension of everyday *civilized* intercourse.

The notion that we can use speech only to talk *about* action, or indirectly to *evoke* action, has dominated modern Western thought. Yet contemporary "linguistic" analysis in philosophy has revealed increasingly how much the ritual word is itself the critical act rather than a report of, or stimulus to, action. The late J. L. Austin was one of those who brought the reality and pervasiveness of this phenomenon to a focus in his analyses of what he called the "performative utterance."[8] These are the innumerable statements we make which function somewhat like the "operative" clause in a legal instrument. They are statements, but they are not statements *about* some act or inviting some action; instead they are the very execution of the act itself.

"I give and bequeath my watch to my brother," duly said or written, is not a report of what I have already done but is the very act of bequeathal itself. In a marriage ceremony, the "I do" is not a report of an inner mental act of acceptance; it is itself the act which seals my part of the bargain. "I promise . . ." is not a report of what I have done a moment before inside my head, nor is it indeed a report of anything at all; the uttering of the words is itself the act of promising. It is by words, and by the ceremony of which the words form a part, that I bind myself in a way which, for a man who really "submits to *li*," is more powerful, more inescapable than strategies or force. Confucius truly tells us that the man who uses the power of *li* can influence those above him—but not the man who has only physical force at his command.

There is no power of *li* if there is no learned and accepted convention, or if we utter the words and invoke the power of the convention in an inappropriate setting, or if the ceremony is not fully carried out, or if the persons carrying out the ceremonial roles are not those properly authorized ("authorization"—again a ceremony). In short, the peculiarly moral yet binding power of ceremonial gesture and word cannot be abstracted from or used in isolation from ceremony. It is not a distinct power we happen to use in ceremony; it is the power *of* ceremony. I cannot effectively go through the ceremony of bequeathing my servant to someone if, in our society, there is no accepted convention of slavery; I cannot bet two dollars if no one completes the bet by accepting; I cannot legally plead "Guilty" to a crime while eating dinner at home. Thus the power of *li* cannot be used except as the *li* is fully respected. This, too, is Confucius' constant refrain. "The Three Families used the Yung Song . . . what possible application can such words have in the Hall of the Three Families?" (who were not entitled, according to *li*, to use this song) (3:2).

For present purposes it is enough to note how many are the obvious performative formulae in our own language and ceremony,[9] and also to note that there may be less obvious but no less important performative formulae—for example, those formulae in which one expresses one's own wish or preference or choice. "I choose this one" excludes the objection, made after one receives it, that one was not speaking truly. For to say it in the proper circumstances is not to report something already done but is to take the "operative" step in making the choice.[10]

The upshot of this approach to language and its "ceremonial" context was, in the reasoning of Austin, paradoxical. He came to feel forced toward the conclusion that ultimately *all* utterances are in some essential way performative. This remains an open question, but it suffices for us to recall that it is now a commonplace of contemporary analytical philosophy (as it was a basic thesis of pragmatist philosophies) that we use words to *do* things, profoundly important and amazingly varied things.

Indeed, the central lesson of these new philosophical insights is not so much a lesson about language as it is about ceremony. What we have come to see, in our own way, is how vast is the area of human existence in which the substance of that existence *is* the ceremony. Promises, commitments, excuses, pleas, compliments, pacts—these and so much more are ceremonies or they are nothing. It is thus in the medium of ceremony that the peculiarly human part of our life is lived. The ceremonial act is the primary, irreducible event; [11] language cannot be understood in isolation from the conventional practice in which it is rooted; conventional practice cannot be understood in isolation from the language which defines and is part of it. No purely physical motion is a promise; no word alone, independent of ceremonial context, circumstances, and roles can be a promise. Word and motion are only abstractions from the concrete ceremonial act.

From this standpoint, it is easy to see that not only motor skills must be learned but also correct use of language. For correct use of language is *constitutive* of effective action as much as gesture is. Correct language is not merely a useful adjunct; it is of the essence of executing the ceremony.

From this perspective we see that the famous Confucian doctrine of *cheng ming*, the "rectification of terms" or "correct use of terminology," is not merely an erroneous belief in word-magic or a pedantic elaboration of Confucius' concern with teaching tradition. Nor do I see any reason to read into it a doctrine of "essences" or Platonic Ideas, or analogous medieval-age neo-Confucian notions, for the *Analects* provides no other hint of any such doctrine.[12]

Of course we must be leery of reading our own contemporary philosophical doctrines into an ancient teaching. Yet I think that the text of the Analects, in letter and spirit, supports and enriches our own quite recently emerging vision of man as a ceremonial being.

In general, what Confucius brings out in connection with the workings of ceremony is not only its distinctively human character, its linguistic and magical character, but also its moral and religious character. Here, finally, we must recall and place at the focus of our analysis the fact that for Confucius it is the imagery of Holy Ceremony which unifies and infuses all these dimensions of human existence. Perhaps a modern Westerner would be tempted to speak of the "intelligent practice of learned conventions and language." This has a fashionably value-free, "scientific" ring. Indeed the contemporary analytical philosophers tend to speak this way and to be suitably common-sensical and restrained in their style. But this quite fails to accomplish what Confucius' central image did.

The image of Holy Rite as a metaphor of human existence brings foremost to our attention the dimension of the holy in man's existence. There are several dimensions of Holy Rite which culminate in its holiness. Rite brings out forcefully not only the harmony and beauty of social forms, the inherent and ultimate dignity of human intercourse; it brings out also the moral perfection implicit in achieving one's ends by dealing with others as beings of equal dignity, as free co-participants in *li*. Furthermore, to act by ceremony is to be completely open to the other; for ceremony is public, shared, transparent; to act otherwise is to be secret, obscure, and devious, or merely tyrannically coercive. It is in this beautiful and dignified, shared and open participation with others who are ultimately like oneself (12:2) that man realizes himself. Thus perfect community of men—the Confucian analogue to Christian brotherhood—becomes an inextricable part, the chief aspect, of divine worship—again an analogy with the central law taught by Jesus.

Confucius wanted to teach us, as a corollary, that sacred ceremony in its narrower, root meaning is not a totally mysterious appeasement of spirits external to human and earthly life. Spirit is no longer an external being influenced by the ceremony; it is that which is expressed and comes most alive *in* the ceremony. Instead of being a diversion of attention from the human realm to another transcendent realm, the overtly holy Ceremony is to be seen as the central symbol, both expressive of and participating in the holy as a dimension of all truly human existence. Explicitly, Holy Rite is thus a luminous point of concentration in the greater and ideally all-inclusive ceremonial harmony of the perfectly humane civilization of the *Tao,* or ideal Way. Human life in its entirety finally appears as one vast, spontaneous and holy Rite: the community of man. This, for Confucius, was indeed an "ultimate concern"; it was, he said again and again, the only thing that mattered, more than the individual's life itself (3:17; 4:5, 6, 8).

NOTES

1. For the purposes of this discussion, I speak of Confucius' thought as if it were in fact the teachings ascribed to him in the *Analects,* especially those portions of the *Analects* which are likely to be earlier and closer to the authentic sayings of Confucius himself. Of course, it has been doubted whether any of the sayings in the *Analects* were actually Confucius', and there seems good reason to suppose that they are at least worked-over versions of his actual words. Nevertheless, the

consensus seems to be that much of the *Analects* constitutes the largest single body of quotations or near-quotations from the historical Confucius. In any case, it is the doctrine to be found in this work that is central to my purpose, not the precise historical origin of it.

As to the identification of this "earliest core" itself, there are differences of opinion. So far as I know, there is a consensus among experts that Chapters 3 through 8 are to be included (certain passages excepted). With individual differences of opinion, there is broadly a consensus that if we go beyond this central core and take larger segments of the work (2–9, 1–9, 1–15, 1–20), we get increasingly great amounts of materials which are later in style and at times, but not always, foreign in content to Confucius' sayings and ideas. I have consulted especially: James Legge, *Confucian Analects in the Chinese Classics* (Hong Kong University Press; reprint, 1960), pp. 12–18; Arthur Waley, *The Analects of Confucius* (New York: Modern Library, 1938), pp. 21–26; H. G. Creel, *Confucius and the Chinese Way* (New York: Harper Torchbook, 1960), pp. 291–294, and his *Literary Chinese by the Inductive Method* (Chicago: University of Chicago Press, 1939), II, 9–21; Daniel Leslie, *Confucius* (Paris: Editions Segher, 1962), pp. 32–35, and his "Notes on the *Analects*," *T'oung Pao,* XLIX (1961); S. Kaizuka, *Confucius,* trans. by G. Bownes (London: George Allen & Unwin, 1956), p. 103.

2. In this middle third of the twelfth century, writers who disagree in many ways almost all tend to agree on the secular, humanist, rationalist orientation of Confucius. Waley says the turn toward the this-worldly was characteristic of tendencies of the age and not peculiar to Confucius (Waley, *op. cit.,* pp. 32–33). See also Leslie, *op. cit.,* pp. 40–41; Wing-tsit Chan, *A Source Book in Chinese Philosophy* (Princeton: Princeton University Press, 1963), p. 15; Creel, *Confucius and the Chinese Way,* p. 120; Kaizuka, *op. cit.,* 109–119; Wu-chi Liu, *Confucius: His Life and Times* (New York: Philosophical Library, 1965), pp. 154–156. Fung Yu-Lan in his various pre-Communist works takes a more ambiguous position on this issue but seems to me to stress the rationalist, humanist aspects, ending by holding this to be a defect of one-sidedness in Confucius; cf. his *The Spirit of Chinese Philosophy,* trans. by E. R. Hughes (Boston: Beacon Press, 1962), p. 28.

3. Quotations from the *Analects* are cited by chapter and paragraph according to the traditional text. There are a number of English translations which follow this order, the two most useful being Legge's and Waley's (cited above, note 1). Legge's is the "classic" English source. Waley's is a modern one, outstanding both in style and scholarship. The quotations as given in this paper are basically Legge's and Waley's with occasional contributions by me.

4. J. L. Duyvendak, "The Philosophy of Wu Wei," *Etudes Asiatiques,* Nos. 3–4 (1947), p. 84.

5. Cf. Waley, *op. cit.,* pp. 64–66, and esp. (p. 66): "I do not think Confucius attributed this magic power to any rites save those practiced by the divinely appointed ruler."

6. See, for example, Waley, *op. cit.,* p. 66.

7. See, for example, Creel, *op. cit.,* pp. 82–83. See also *Analects,* 9:3.

8. J. L. Austin, "Performative Utterances," in *Philosophical Papers* (London: Oxford University Press, 1961), pp. 220–239; *How to Do Things with Words* (London: Oxford University Press, 1962); "Performatif-Constantif," in *La Philosophie Analytique, Cahiers de Royaumont,* Phil. No. IV (Paris: Editions de Minuit, 1962), pp. 271–305.

9. Though the list could go on interminably, I mention here just a few more terms which commonly enter into formulae having an obvious performative function: "I christen you," "I appoint you," "I pick this (or him)," "I congratulate you," "I welcome you," "I authorize you," "I challenge you," "I order you," "I request you."

10. For an extensive and characteristic example of the recent trend to treat as a special, crucial category these and other first-person present-tense expressions using "mental" or "action" verbs, see S. Hampshire, *Thought and Action* (London: Chatto & Windus, 1959).

11. The literature on issues pertaining to this topic is now vast, and in general one might summarize by saying that there are two distinct and contrasting trends, easily the two most influential throughout the English-speaking philosophical world. One trend is the "formalistic" analysis of science, language, and "knowledge," a kind of analysis which, in a much more attenuated and sophisticated way, still leans toward a view, opposed to what I have here expressed, which denies the ultimate irreducibility of such notions as, e.g., "the ceremonial act," and argues instead for a behavioral or physicalist approach to human conduct. I have in mind here the movement inspired by Russell and Whitehead's *Principia Mathematica* and by the work of the "Vienna Circle"; the more specific and recent tendencies may be sampled in such standard anthologies as that of H. Feigl and M. Brodbeck, *Readings in the Philosophy of Science* (New York: Appleton-Century-Crofts, 1953); and in the series "Minnesota Studies in Philosophy of Science." The other trend has its roots in the later work of L. Wittgenstein, G. Ryle, J. L. Austin, P. F. Strawson, John Wisdom, and others. These analysts have concentrated on the natural languages (hence not "formal" languages), and have in one way or another argued that the physicalist-behavioralist approaches to "mind" and "action" are fundamentally misconceived. They have been elaborating in great detail alternative analyses

which, though not identical, have family resemblances and which affirm a radical logical gap between the language of "action," "mind," and, in effect, what I have here called the ceremonial act, and on the other hand the mathematical-physical language of physical science.

12. This position is taken more or less explicitly in the various works of Fung Yu-Lan. The *Analects* passage which is most explicit—indeed the only fully explicit passage on *cheng ming* in the *Analects* (13:3)—is evidently much later in style than and different in content from the core of the work (see Waley, *op. cit.*, p. 172). Even so, the passage does not itself say that names must "correspond" to "actualities" (Fung, *op. cit.*, p. 60; also essentially Chu Hsi's interpretation in his commentary on the *Lun Yu*). Nor does it say names must be "in accordance with the truth" (Legge), nor that "language must concord with what is meant" (Waley). The text itself merely says that names (or language) must be concordant (what is needed, or what goes with). But this leaves it ambiguous: must language be concordant with the activity (*li*) of which it is a part ("the prince *being* a prince"), or must it concord as name with thing named? My own view is that the distinction was not originally clear, and that both senses were tacitly in mind. Even in Hsun Tzu, if one reads carefully with this question in mind, the issue is not clearly formulated one way or another, though he is always read as if he were definitely speaking of name and thing named. But this is in large part due to our own Western bias toward this traditional (but now widely rejected) doctrine of how language works; it is supported by the analogous view which also developed in China and becomes part of the orthodox commentary. Once we are aware of the ceremonial or performative kinds of functions of language, the original texts begin to read differently.

Acknowledgments

Chapter 2, "Acceptance of Responsibility," originally appeared, under the title "Responsibility," in *Mind: A Quarterly Review of Psychology and Philosophy,* LXXV, N.S., No. 297 (January 1966), 58–74.

Chapter 3, "Self-Insight as Self-Discovery, Self-Realization, Self-Creation," originally appeared, under the title "A Fresh Perspective on a Familiar Landscape," in the *Journal of Humanistic Psychology,* II (Spring 1962), 75–89.

Chapter 4, "Real Guilt and Neurotic Guilt," originally appeared in the *Journal of Existential Psychiatry,* III (1962), 145–158.

Chapter 5, "From Oedipus to Orestes: A Paradigm of Becoming Responsible," originally appeared, under the title "Orestes: Paradigm Hero and Central Motif of Contemporary Ego Psychology," in *The Psychoanalytic Review,* Fall 1963, pp. 87–111.

Chapter 6, "The Good Samaritan and the Law," was originally prepared as a paper for the University of Chicago School of Law symposium "The Good Samaritan and the Bad" (1965); subsequently printed, under the title "Some Moral Aspects of Good Samaritanship," in James M. Ratcliffe (ed.), *The Good Samaritan and the Law* (New York: Doubleday-Anchor, 1966), pp. 213–223.

Chapter 7, "Human Community as Holy Rite: An Interpretation of Confucius' *Analects,*" originally appeared in *The Harvard Theological Review,* LIX, No. 1 (January 1966), 53–67.